the inspired
vegetarian

the inspired
vegetarian

CREATIVE IDEAS FOR
NATURAL, HEALTHY EATING

CHRISTINE INGRAM

LORENZ BOOKS

This edition published by Lorenz Books
27 West 20th Street, New York, NY 10011

LORENZ BOOKS are available for bulk purchase for sales promotion
and for premium use. For details, write or call the sales director,
Lorenz Books, 27 West 20th Street, New York, NY 10011;
(800) 354-9657

ISBN 1 85967 835 1

Publisher: Joanna Lorenz
Designers: Patrick McLeavy and Siân Keogh
Photography and styling: Patrick McLeavy and Tom Odulate

Front cover: Lisa Tai, Designer; Thomas Odulate, Photographer;
Helen Trent, Stylist; Marie-Ange Lapierre, Home Economist

Previously published as part of a larger compendium, *The Complete Encyclopedia of Vegetables and Vegetarian Cooking*

Printed and bound in Hong Kong/China

© Anness Publishing Limited 1998, 1999
Updated © 2000
1 3 5 7 9 10 8 6 4 2

NOTES

Standard spoon and cup measures are level.

CONTENTS

~

INTRODUCTION

Committed vegetarians know that a diet excluding meat and fish need not be boring, but perhaps few people realize just how appetizing and attractive vegetarian dishes can be. This book is packed with truly superb recipes for special occasions. Even if your guests are normally committed meat-eaters, they will be delighted by any of these succulent dishes, and friends who are already vegetarians will be amazed by their range and variety.

Vegetables may play the starring role in a recipe or they may be combined with other ingredients, such as rice or pasta. These sorts of dishes are loved for the harmony of their flavor, rather than for the taste of the individual vegetables from which they have been made. However, you will also find many recipes in the following pages that make the most of particular vegetables, so that the specific virtues of each can be appreciated to the full. There is a mix of classic dishes from around the world, such as Gazpacho, Italian Roast Peppers, Hot Sour Chickpeas, and Greek Stuffed Vegetables, together with others that have been devised to make the most of individual ingredients. Try, for example, Roast Asparagus Crêpes, Spinach Ravioli, Baked Marrow in Parsley Sauce, or Vegetables Julienne with a Red Pepper Coulis.

The book is divided into four chapters: Soups & Appetizers, Light Lunches, Suppers, and Salads & Side Dishes. All the recipes are vegetarian and many are suitable for vegans. They are all very flexible and can easily be adapted to include your own favorite ingredients or vegetables in season. All look tempting and there is something suitable for every occasion when you are entertaining, whether your neighbors are joining you for a weekend brunch, you are giving a formal dinner party or enjoying a special family gathering.

THE VEGETARIAN PANTRY

The basis of the vegetarian diet is, of course, formed by vegetables of all kinds. However, many other ingredients are required, both for their individual culinary qualities and for a healthy, balanced diet. There can easily be a shortfall of some essential nutrients, such as iron, in the vegetarian diet, and vegans need to be especially scrupulous about including a wide variety of different foods.

FLOURS

Have a selection of different flours to ring the changes. Often it is a good idea to mix two types together in baking for flavor and texture. Use half whole-wheat and half white flours for a lighter brown pastry crust. Mix buckwheat flour with white for crêpes. Flour is a good source of protein, as well as complex starchy carbohydrate. Brown/whole-wheat flours do not keep as long as more refined flours.

RICE

The best rice is basmati, an elegant, fragrant, long grain rice, grown in the foothills of the Himalayas. Traditionally eaten with curries, basmati is marvelous in almost all savory rice dishes. Brown basmati is a lighter wholegrain rice with higher levels of dietary fiber. Thai rices are delicate and lightly sticky, making them particularly good in stir-fries. Wild rice, which is actually an aquatic grass, has good levels of protein. Italian risotto rices have shorter grains and can absorb a great deal of liquid without becoming soggy, creating the desired creamy texture.

PASTA

The mainstay of many a cook in a hurry, pasta is also a good source of complex carbohydrates, and it is available in a multitude of shapes, colors, and flavors. Pasta should be cooked until it is tender, but still firm to the bite. Choose pasta that is made from durum wheat or durum semolina. Cook it in plenty of lightly salted boiling water, according to the packet instructions, and drain well.

PULSES

Over half the world's main source of protein comes from pulses in one form or another. However, although high in protein, pulses are not complete in all amino acids. Grains, too, lack some amino acids, but by combining pulses and grains, you can complete the protein circle.

Dried pulses benefit from being soaked in cold water overnight. A shortcut is to cover them with boiling water and soak for 2 hours. Drain and cook in fresh water. Boil pulses vigorously for the first 10 minutes of cooking to destroy naturally occurring toxins. Then lower the heat and gently simmer. Do not add salt or lemon juice during cooking, as this toughens the skins, although herbs and perhaps slices of onion will add flavor. Drain  the cooked pulses, but do not dry out completely.

Certain lentils can be cooked without pre-soaking. The small, split red lentils, masoor dhal, are marvelous for sprinkling in as thickeners for soups and stews, and take just 20 minutes to cook. Beans 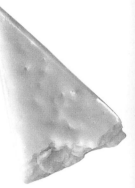 with a good creamy texture that is perfect for soups, pâtés, and purées are lima beans, kidney beans, cannellini, navy, borlotti, pinto, and flageolets. Split peas and red lentils make good dips. Chickpeas and aduki beans hold their texture well during cooking and make a good base for burgers and stews.

CHEESE

This is a popular high-protein food with vegetarians, although not, of course, with vegans who do not eat dairy products. It is very high in calories compared with many other carbohydrate and protein foods. As it is so easy to incorporate in the vegetarian diet, there is a temptation to use it quite heavily, and it is important to watch the intake of this potentially high cholesterol product.

For fuller flavor, choose aged varieties of cheese, such as sharp farmhouse Cheddar or fresh Parmesan—you will then not need to use so much. Leave some full-flavored cheese unwrapped in the refrigerator to dry out: this concentrates the flavor and makes it go further when it is finely grated.

Among the most useful cheeses are sharp Cheddar, fresh Parmesan, Swiss cheese, and pecorino. Lower-fat soft cheese and goat cheeses are ideal for stirring into hot food to make an instant, tasty, creamy sauce.

OTHER DAIRY PRODUCTS

Supermarkets carry a wide range of cultured dairy goods, which present many exciting opportunities to the home cook. Crème fraîche is a French-style sour cream which does not curdle when boiled, so it is ideal stirred into hot dishes. However, like heavy cream, it is quite high in fat (40 per cent), so use it sparingly.

Unsweetened yogurt is a smooth, slightly tangy, lower-fat, creamy product that is ideal for dressings and baked potatoes.

Curd, cream, and cottage cheeses are long-time favorites and are now available in lower-fat versions.

DAIRY-FREE PRODUCTS

The unassuming soybean is one of the best sources of high vegetable protein foods. It is ideal as a base for dairy-free milks, creams, spreads, and cheeses, making it perfect for vegans and those with dairy product allergies. Use these in the same way as their dairy product counterparts, although anyone coming newly to them will find that soy products taste slightly sweeter.

Bean curd, also known as tofu, is made with soy milk and is particularly versatile in vegetarian cooking, both as a main ingredient in recipes or to add creamy, firm texture. On its own, tofu has little flavor, making it ideal to use as an absorber of other flavors. This is why it is so popular in Asian cooking. Firm bean curd or tofu can be cut

into cubes, marinated, or smoked. It is very good fried in oil or broiled to a crisp, golden crust.

A softer set bean curd, called silken bean curd, is a good substitute for cream and can be stirred into hot soups and used as a base filling for baked flans. Indeed, any time when a recipe calls for milk or cream, it can be used instead.

Not only high in protein, bean curd is a good source of iron and vitamins of the B group. (Remember to serve some vitamin C during the same meal to enable the body to make use of a vegetable source of iron.)

Mycoprotein (brand name Quorn) is a manmade food, distantly related to the mushroom. Low in fat and calories, it is high in protein and has as much fiber as green vegetables. It cooks quickly, absorbing flavors as easily as soybean curd, but has a firmer texture. It is good for stir-frying, stews, and casseroles.

NUTS AND SEEDS

Not only are they full of flavor, texture, and color, but nuts and seeds are great nutritional power packs. However, they can be high in fats as well as proteins.

Cheapest and most versatile are peanuts, which are best bought unsalted. Almonds are also very useful, as are walnuts, pine nuts,

hazelnuts, and the more expensive cashews. Mixing two or three types together can be very successful.

Nuts go rancid if they are stored for more than about six months, so if you do not use them regularly, buy only small quantities. For maximum flavor, lightly roast nuts before chopping or crushing.

An increasing range of seeds is now available from supermarkets and wholefood stores. Most useful are sunflower and sesame seeds, while pumpkin and melon seeds are very attractive scattered into salads or nibbled with pre-dinner drinks. Seeds for an attractive garnish as well as flavor include poppy, black mustard, fenugreek, and caraway seeds.

HERBS

Whenever possible, try to use fresh herbs. Do not use just one herb per dish: mix and match, experimenting with different combinations. Although you should not skimp on herbs, the more pungent ones, such as tarragon, rosemary, and sage, should be used with discretion. Particularly useful herbs are parsley, cilantro, dill, basil, chives, and mint. If you have to use dried herbs, buy small quantities.

SOUPS &
APPETIZERS

~

PEAR AND WATERCRESS SOUP WITH STILTON CROUTONS

PEARS AND STILTON TASTE VERY GOOD WHEN EATEN TOGETHER AFTER THE MAIN COURSE. HERE, FOR A CHANGE, THEY ARE COMBINED IN AN APPETIZER.

SERVES SIX

INGREDIENTS
  1 bunch watercress
  4 medium pears, sliced
  3¾ cups vegetable stock
  salt and pepper
  ½ cup heavy cream
  juice of 1 lime
For the croutons
  2 tablespoons butter
  1 tablespoon olive oil
  3 cups stale bread, cubed
  1 cup chopped Stilton cheese

1 Set aside about one-third of the watercress leaves. Place all the rest of the leaves and the stalks in a pan with the pears, stock and a little seasoning. Simmer for about 15–20 minutes. Reserving a few watercress leaves for garnish, add the rest and immediately blend in a food processor until smooth.

2 Put the mixture in a bowl and stir in the cream and lime juice to mix the flavors thoroughly. Season again to taste. Pour all the soup back into a pan and reheat, stirring until warmed through.

3 To make the croutons, melt the butter and oil in a pan and fry the bread cubes until golden brown. Drain on paper towels. Put the cheese on top, then heat under a hot broiler until bubbling.

4 Pour the reheated soup into bowls. Use the croutons and remaining watercress leaves to garnish the soup before serving.

ASPARAGUS SOUP

HOME-MADE ASPARAGUS SOUP HAS A DELICATE FLAVOR, QUITE UNLIKE THAT FROM A CAN. THIS SOUP IS BEST MADE WITH YOUNG ASPARAGUS, WHICH IS TENDER AND BLENDS WELL. SERVE IT WITH WAFER-THIN SLICES OF BREAD.

SERVES FOUR

INGREDIENTS
    1 pound young asparagus
    1½ ounces butter
    6 shallots, sliced
    ½ ounce all-purpose flour
    2½ cups vegetable stock or water
    1 tablespoon lemon juice
    1 cup milk
    ½ cup light cream
    2 teaspoons chopped fresh chervil
    salt and freshly ground black pepper

1 Trim the stalks of the asparagus if necessary. Cut 1½ inches off the tops of half the asparagus and set aside for a garnish. Slice the remaining asparagus.

2 Melt 1 ounce of the butter in a large saucepan and gently fry the sliced shallots for 2–3 minutes until soft but not brown, stirring occasionally.

3 Add the sliced asparagus and fry over low heat for about 1 minute. Stir in the flour, cook for 1 minute. Stir in the stock or water, lemon juice and season to taste. Bring to a boil and then simmer, partially covered, for 15–20 minutes until the asparagus is very tender.

4 Cool slightly and then process the soup in a food processor or blender until smooth. Then press the puréed asparagus through a strainer placed over a clean saucepan. Add the milk by pouring and stirring it through the strainer with the asparagus so as to extract the maximum amount of asparagus purée.

5 Melt the remaining butter and fry the reserved asparagus tips gently for about 3–4 minutes to soften.

6 Heat the soup gently for 3–4 minutes. Stir in the cream and the asparagus tips. Heat gently and serve sprinkled with the chopped fresh chervil.

CLASSIC MINESTRONE

*THE HOMEMADE VERSION OF THIS
FAMOUS SOUP IS A DELICIOUS
REVELATION AND MOUTH-
WATERINGLY HEALTHY.*

SERVES FOUR

INGREDIENTS
  1 large leek, thinly sliced
  2 carrots, chopped
  1 zucchini, thinly sliced
  4 ounces whole green beans, halved
  2 stalks celery, thinly sliced
  3 tablespoons olive oil
  6 cups vegetable stock
  1 can (14 ounces) tomatoes, chopped
  1 tablespoon fresh basil, chopped
  1 teaspoon chopped fresh thyme
    leaves, or ½ teaspoon dried thyme
  salt and freshly ground black pepper
  1 can (14 ounces) cannellini
    or kidney beans
  ⅓ cup small pasta shapes or macaroni
  fresh Parmesan cheese, finely grated
    (optional) and fresh parsley, chopped,
    to garnish

1 Put all the fresh vegetables in a large
saucepan with the olive oil. Heat until
sizzling, then cover, lower the heat and
sweat the vegetables for 15 minutes,
shaking the pan occasionally.

2 Add the stock (use water if desired),
tomatoes, herbs and seasoning. Bring to a
boil, replace the lid and simmer gently for
about 30 minutes.

3 Add the beans and their liquor together
with the pasta, and simmer for another
10 minutes. Check the seasoning and
serve hot, sprinkled with the Parmesan
cheese (if using) and parsley.

COOK'S TIP
Minestrone is also delicious served cold
on a hot summer's day. In fact, the flavor
improves if it is made a day or two ahead
and stored in the refrigerator. It can also
be frozen and reheated.

GAZPACHO

Gazpacho is a classic Spanish soup. It is popular all over Spain but nowhere more so than in Andalucia, where there are hundreds of variations. It is a cold soup of tomatoes, tomato juice, green bell pepper and garlic, which is served with a selection of garnishes.

SERVES FOUR

INGREDIENTS
   3–3½ pounds ripe tomatoes
   1 green bell pepper, seeded and
      roughly chopped
   2 garlic cloves, crushed
   2 slices white bread, crusts removed
   4 tablespoons olive oil
   4 tablespoons tarragon wine vinegar
   ⅔ cup tomato juice
   good pinch of sugar
   salt and freshly ground black pepper
   ice cubes, to serve·
For the garnishes
   2 tablespoons sunflower oil
   2–3 slices white bread, diced
   1 small cucumber, peeled and
      finely diced
   1 small onion, finely chopped
   1 red bell pepper, seeded and finely diced
   1 green bell pepper, seeded and finely
      diced
   2 hard-boiled eggs, chopped

1 Skin the tomatoes, then quarter them and remove the cores.

2 Place the pepper in a food processor and process for a few seconds. Add the tomatoes, garlic, bread, olive oil and vinegar and process again. Add the tomato juice, sugar, seasoning and a little extra tomato juice or cold water and process. The consistency should be thick but not too stodgy.

3 Pour into a bowl and chill for at least 2 hours but no more than 12 hours, otherwise the textures deteriorate.

4 To prepare the bread cubes to use as a garnish, heat the oil in a frying pan and fry them until golden brown. Drain well.

5 Place each garnish in a separate small dish, or alternately arrange them in rows on a large plate.

6 Just before serving, stir a few ice cubes into the soup and then spoon into serving bowls. Serve with the garnishes.

WINTER WARMER SOUP

SIMMER A VARIETY OF WINTER ROOT VEGETABLES TOGETHER FOR A WARMING AND SATISFYING SOUP.

SERVES SIX

INGREDIENTS

    3 medium carrots, chopped
    1 large potato, chopped
    1 large parsnip, chopped
    1 large turnip or small rutabaga, chopped
    1 onion, chopped
    2 tablespoons sunflower oil
    2 tablespoons butter
    6 cups water
    salt and freshly ground black pepper
    1 piece fresh ginger, grated
    1¼ cups milk
    3 tablespoons sour cream or plain
      yogurt
    2 tablespoons chopped fresh dill
    fresh lemon juice

1 Put the carrots, potato, parsnip, turnip or rutabaga and onion into a large saucepan with the oil and butter. Fry lightly, then cover and sweat the vegetables over very low heat for 15 minutes, shaking the pan occasionally.

2 Pour in the water, bring to a boil and season well. Cover and simmer for 20 minutes, until the vegetables are soft.

3 Strain the vegetables, reserving the stock, add the ginger and purée in a food processor or blender until smooth.

4 Return the purée and stock to the pan. Add the milk and stir while the soup gently reheats.

5 Remove from the heat, stir in the sour cream or yogurt plus the dill, lemon juice and extra seasoning, if necessary. Reheat the soup, if desired, but do not allow it to boil as you do so, or it may curdle.

GARLIC MUSHROOMS

GARLIC AND MUSHROOMS MAKE A WONDERFUL COMBINATION. THEY MUST BE SERVED PIPING HOT, SO IF POSSIBLE USE A BALTI PAN OR CAST-IRON FRYING PAN AND DON'T STAND ON CEREMONY — SERVE STRAIGHT FROM THE PAN.

SERVES FOUR (as a starter)

INGREDIENTS
   2 tablespoons sunflower oil
   1 ounce butter
   5 scallions, thinly sliced
   3 garlic cloves, crushed
   1 pound white mushrooms
   1½ ounces fresh white bread crumbs
   1 tablespoon chopped fresh parsley
   2 tablespoons lemon juice
   salt and freshly ground black pepper

1 Heat the oil and butter in a balti pan, wok or cast-iron frying pan. Add the scallions and garlic and stir-fry over medium heat for 1–2 minutes.

2 Add the whole white mushrooms and fry over high heat for 4–5 minutes, stirring and tossing with a large wide spatula or wooden spoon, all the time.

3 Stir in the bread crumbs, parsley, lemon juice and seasoning. Stir-fry for a few minutes until the lemon juice has virtually evaporated and then serve.

ROAST GARLIC WITH CROÛTONS

YOUR GUESTS WILL BE ASTONISHED TO BE SERVED A WHOLE ROAST GARLIC FOR A STARTER. ROAST GARLIC HAS A HEAVENLY FLAVOR AND IS SO IRRESISTIBLE THAT THEY WILL EVEN FORGIVE YOU THE NEXT DAY!

SERVES FOUR

INGREDIENTS
   2 garlic bulbs
   3 tablespoons olive oil
   3 tablespoons water
   sprig of rosemary
   sprig of thyme
   1 bay leaf
   sea salt and freshly ground
     black pepper
To serve
   slices of Italian bread
   olive or sunflower oil, for frying
   6 ounces young goat cheese or soft
     cream cheese
   2 tablespoons chopped fresh herbs,
     e.g. marjoram, parsley and chives

1 Preheat the oven to 375°F. Place the garlic bulbs in a small ovenproof dish and pour over the oil and water. Add the rosemary, thyme and bay leaf and sprinkle with sea salt and pepper. Cover with foil and bake in the oven for 30 minutes.

2 Remove the foil, baste the garlic heads with the juices from the dish and bake for a further 15–20 minutes until they feel soft when pressed.

3 Heat a little oil in a frying pan and fry the Italian bread on both sides until golden. Blend the cheese with the mixed herbs and place in a serving dish.

4 Cut each garlic bulb in half and open out slightly. Serve the garlic on small plates with the croûtons and soft cheese. Each garlic clove should be squeezed out of its papery shell, spread over a croûton and eaten with the cheese.

GUACAMOLE

THIS IS QUITE A FIERY VERSION OF A POPULAR MEXICAN DISH, ALTHOUGH PROBABLY NOWHERE NEAR AS HOT AS YOU WOULD BE SERVED IN MEXICO, WHERE IT SEEMS HEAT KNOWS NO BOUNDS!

SERVES FOUR

INGREDIENTS

2 ripe avocados, peeled and pitted
2 tomatoes, peeled, seeded and finely chopped
6 scallions, finely chopped
1–2 chilies, seeded and finely chopped
2 tablespoons fresh lime or lemon juice
1 tablespoon chopped fresh cilantro
salt and freshly ground black pepper
coriander sprig, to garnish

1 Put the avocado halves into a bowl and mash roughly with a large fork.

2 Add the remaining ingredients. Mix well and season according to taste. Serve garnished with fresh cilantro.

ARUGULA AND GRILLED GOAT CHEESE SALAD

GOAT CHEESE CAN BE BOUGHT IN MANY DIFFERENT FORMS. FOR THIS RECIPE, LOOK OUT FOR CYLINDER-SHAPED GOAT CHEESE FROM A DELICATESSEN OR FOR SMALL ROLLS THAT CAN BE CUT INTO PIECES WEIGHING ABOUT 2 OUNCES.

SERVES FOUR

INGREDIENTS
    about 1 tablespoon olive oil
    about 1 tablespoon vegetable oil
    4 slices Italian bread
    3 tablespoons walnut oil
    1 tablespoon lemon juice
    8-ounce cylinder-shape goat cheese
    generous handful of arugula leaves
    about 4 ounces frisée
For the sauce
    3 tablespoons apricot jam
    4 tablespoons white wine
    2 teaspoons Dijon mustard

1 Heat the olive and vegetable oils in a frying pan and fry the slices of Italian bread on one side only, until lightly golden brown. Transfer to a plate lined with paper towels.

4 Preheat the broiler a few minutes before serving the salad. Cut the goat cheese into 2-ounce rounds and place each piece on a croûton, untoasted side up. Place under the broiler and cook for 3–4 minutes until the cheese melts.

5 Toss the arugula and frisée in the walnut oil dressing and arrange attractively on four individual serving plates. When the croûtons are ready, arrange on each plate and pour over a little of the apricot sauce.

2 To make the sauce, heat the jam in a small saucepan until warm but not boiling. Push through a strainer, into a clean pan, to remove the pieces of fruit, and then stir in the white wine and mustard. Heat gently and then keep warm until ready to serve.

3 Blend the walnut oil and lemon juice and season with a little salt and pepper.

MUSHROOMS ON TOAST

SERVE THESE ON TOAST FOR A QUICK, TASTY STARTER OR POP THEM INTO SMALL RAMEKINS AND SERVE WITH SLICES OF WARM CRUSTY BREAD. USE SOME SHITAKE MUSHROOMS, IF YOU CAN FIND THEM, FOR A RICHER FLAVOR.

SERVES FOUR

INGREDIENTS
    1 pound white mushrooms, sliced if large
    3 tablespoons olive oil
    3 tablespoons vegetable stock or water
    2 tablespoons dry sherry (optional)
    3 garlic cloves, crushed
    4 ounces low-fat cream cheese
    2 tablespoons chopped fresh parsley
    1 tablespoon chopped fresh chives
    salt and freshly ground black pepper

1 Put the mushrooms into a large saucepan with the olive oil, stock or water and sherry, if using. Heat until bubbling then cover and simmer for 5 minutes.

2 Add the garlic and stir well. Cook for another 2 minutes. Remove the mushrooms with a slotted spoon and set them aside. Cook the liquor until it reduces down to 2 tablespoons. Remove from the heat and stir in the cheese and herbs.

3 Stir the mixture well until the cheese melts, then return the mushrooms to the pan so that they become coated with the cheese mixture. Season to taste.

4 Pile the mushrooms onto thick slabs of hot toast. Alternatively, spoon them into four ramekins and serve accompanied by slices of crusty bread.

RICOTTA AND PINTO BEAN PÂTÉ

FOR AN ATTRACTIVE PRESENTATION, SPOON THE PÂTÉ INTO SMALL, OILED RING MOLDS, TURN OUT AND FILL WITH WHOLE BORLOTTI BEANS, DRESSED WITH LEMON JUICE, OLIVE OIL AND FRESH HERBS.

SERVES FOUR

INGREDIENTS
    1 can (14 ounces) pinto beans, drained
    1 garlic clove, crushed
    1 cup ricotta cheese,
      or cream cheese
    ¼ cup butter, melted
    juice of ½ lemon
    salt and freshly ground black pepper
    2 tablespoons chopped fresh parsley
    1 tablespoon chopped fresh thyme
      or dill
To serve
    extra canned beans (optional)
    fresh lemon juice, olive oil and
      chopped herbs (optional)
    lettuce leaves, radish slices and a few
      sprigs fresh dill, to garnish

1 Blend the beans, garlic, cheese, butter, lemon juice and seasoning in a food processor until smooth.

2 Add the chopped herbs and continue to blend. Spoon into one serving dish or four lightly oiled ramekins, the bottoms lined with discs of waxed paper. Chill the pâté so that it sets firm.

3 If serving with extra beans, dress them with lemon juice, olive oil and herbs, season well and spoon on top. Garnish with lettuce leaves and serve with warm crusty bread or toast.

4 If serving individually, turn each pâté out of its ramekin onto a small plate and remove the disc of paper. Top with radish slices and sprigs of dill.

VARIATION
You could try other canned pulses for this recipe, although the softer lentils would not be suitable. Lima beans are surprisingly good. For an attractive presentation, fill the center with dark red kidney beans and chopped fresh green beans.

ARTICHOKES WITH GARLIC AND HERB BUTTER

IT IS FUN EATING ARTICHOKES AND EVEN MORE FUN TO SHARE ONE BETWEEN TWO PEOPLE. YOU CAN ALWAYS HAVE A SECOND ONE TO FOLLOW SO THAT YOU GET YOUR FAIR SHARE!

SERVES FOUR

INGREDIENTS
  2 artichokes
  salt
For the garlic and herb butter
  3 ounces butter
  1 garlic clove, crushed
  1 tablespoon mixed chopped fresh
    tarragon, marjoram and parsley

1 Wash the artichokes well in cold water. Using a sharp knife cut off the stalks level with the bases. Cut off the top ½ inch of leaves. Snip off the pointed ends of the remaining leaves with scissors.

2 Put the prepared artichokes in a large saucepan of lightly salted water. Bring to a boil, cover and cook for about 40–45 minutes or until a lower leaf comes away easily when gently pulled.

3 Drain upside down for a couple of minutes while making the sauce. Melt the butter over low heat, add the garlic and cook for 30 seconds. Remove from the heat, stir in the herbs and then pour into one or two small serving bowls.

4 Place the artichokes on serving plates and serve with the garlic and herb butter.

COOK'S TIP
To eat an artichoke, pull off each leaf and dip into the garlic and herb butter. Scrape off the soft fleshy base with your teeth. When the center is reached, pull out the hairy choke and discard it, as it is inedible. The base can be cut up and eaten with the remaining garlic butter.

PLANTAIN APPETIZER

PLANTAINS ARE A TYPE OF COOKING BANANA WITH A LOWER SUGAR CONTENT THAN DESSERT BANANAS. THEY ARE UNSUITABLE FOR EATING RAW AND CAN BE USED IN A WIDE RANGE OF DISHES. THIS DELICIOUS ASSORTMENT OF SWEET AND SAVORY PLANTAINS IS A POPULAR DISH IN AFRICA.

SERVES FOUR

INGREDIENTS
  2 green plantains
  3 tablespoons vegetable oil
  1 small onion, very thinly sliced
  1 yellow plantain
  ½ garlic clove, crushed
  salt and cayenne pepper
  vegetable oil, for frying

1 Peel one of the green plantains and cut into wafer-thin rounds, preferably using a swivel-headed potato peeler.

2 Heat about 1 tablespoon of the oil in a large frying pan and fry the plantain slices for 2–3 minutes until golden, turning occasionally. Transfer to a plate lined with paper towels and keep warm.

3 Coarsely grate the other green plantain and mix with the onion.

4 Heat 1 tablespoon of the remaining oil in the pan and fry the plantain and onion mixture for 2–3 minutes until golden, turning occasionally. Transfer to the plate with the plantain slices.

5 Peel the yellow plantain, cut into small chunks. Sprinkle with cayenne pepper. Heat the remaining oil and fry the yellow plantain and garlic for 4–5 minutes until brown. Drain and sprinkle with salt.

MEDITERRANEAN VEGETABLES WITH TAHINI

WONDERFULLY COLORFUL, THIS APPETIZER IS EASILY PREPARED IN ADVANCE. TAHINI IS A PASTE MADE FROM SESAME SEEDS.

SERVES FOUR

INGREDIENTS
  2 bell peppers, seeded and quartered
  2 zucchini, halved lengthwise
  2 small eggplants, halved lengthwise,
    and degorged (see Cook's Tip)
  1 fennel bulb, quartered
  olive oil
  salt and freshly ground black pepper
  4 ounces Greek Halloumi cheese, sliced
For the tahini cream
  1 cup tahini paste
  1 garlic cloves, crushed
  2 tablespoons olive oil
  2 tablespoons fresh lemon juice
  ½ cup cold water

1 Preheat the broiler or barbecue until hot. Brush the vegetables with the oil and broil until just browned, turning once. (If the peppers blacken, don't worry. The skins can be peeled off.) Cook the vegetables until just softened.

2 Place the vegetables in a shallow dish and season. Let cool. Meanwhile, brush the cheese slices with oil and broil or grill on both sides until just charred. Remove them with a spatula.

3 To make the tahini cream, place all the ingredients, except the water, in a food processor or blender. Pulse for a few seconds to mix, then, with the motor still running, pour in the water and blend until smooth.

4 Serve the vegetables and cheese on a platter and drizzle the cream on top of them. Delicious served with warm pita pockets or naan.

COOK'S TIP
To degorge eggplants, sprinkle cut slices with salt and let the juices that form drain away in a colander. After 30 minutes or so, rinse well and pat dry. Degorged eggplants are less bitter and easier to cook.

DOLMADES

DOLMADES ARE STUFFED VINE LEAVES, A TRADITIONAL GREEK DISH. IF YOU CAN'T OBTAIN FRESH VINE LEAVES, USE A PACKET OF BRINED VINE LEAVES. SOAK THE LEAVES IN HOT WATER FOR 20 MINUTES THEN RINSE AND DRY WELL ON PAPER TOWELS BEFORE USE.

MAKES 20–24

INGREDIENTS

20–30 fresh young vine leaves
2 tablespoons olive oil
1 large onion, finely chopped
1 garlic clove, crushed
8 ounces cooked long grain rice,
  or mixed white and wild rice
about 3 tablespoons pine nuts
1 tablespoon slivered almonds
1½ ounces golden raisins
15ml/ 1 tablespoon snipped chives
1 tablespoon finely chopped
  fresh mint
juice of ½ lemon
⅔ cup white wine
hot vegetable stock
salt and freshly ground black pepper
sprig of mint, to garnish
Greek yogurt, to serve

1 Bring a large pan of water to a boil and cook the vine leaves for about 2–3 minutes. They will darken and go limp after about 1 minute and simmering for a further minute or so ensures they are pliable. If using leaves from a packet, place them in a large bowl, cover with boiling water and leave for a few minutes until the leaves can be easily separated. Rinse them under cold water and drain on paper towels.

2 Heat the oil in a small frying pan and fry the onion and garlic for 3–4 minutes over low heat until soft.

3 Spoon the onion and garlic mixture into a bowl and add the cooked rice,

4 Stir in 2 tablespoons of the pine nuts, the almonds, golden raisins, chives, mint, lemon juice and seasoning and mix well.

5 Lay a vine leaf on a clean work surface, veined side uppermost. Place a spoonful of filling near the stem, fold the lower part of the leaf over it and roll up, folding in the sides as you go. Continue stuffing the vine leaves in the same way.

6 Line the bottom of a deep frying pan with four large vine leaves. Place the stuffed vine leaves close together in the pan, seam side down, in a single layer.

7 Add the wine and enough stock to just cover the vine leaves. Place a plate directly over the leaves, then cover and simmer gently for 30 minutes, checking to make sure the pan does not boil dry.

8 Chill the vine leaves garnished with the remaining pine nuts and a sprig of mint and serve with a little yogurt.

BRUSCHETTA WITH GOAT'S CHEESE AND TAPENADE

SIMPLE TO PREPARE IN ADVANCE, THIS APPEALING DISH CAN BE SERVED AS AN APPETIZER OR AT FINGER BUFFETS.

SERVES FOUR TO SIX

INGREDIENTS

For the tapenade
- 1 can (14 ounces) pitted black olives, finely chopped
- ¼ cup chopped sun-dried tomatoes in oil
- 2 tablespoons capers, chopped
- 1 tablespoon green peppercorns in brine, crushed
- 3–4 tablespoons olive oil
- 2 garlic cloves, crushed
- 3 tablespoons chopped, fresh basil, or 1 teaspoon dried basil
- salt and freshly ground black pepper

For the bases
- 12 slices ciabatta or other crusty bread
- olive oil, for brushing
- 2 garlic cloves, halved
- 4 ounces soft goat cheese
- fresh herb sprigs, to garnish

1 Mix all the tapenade ingredients together and check the seasoning. It should not need too much. Let marinate overnight, if possible.

2 To make the bruschetta, broil both sides of the bread lightly until golden. Brush one side with oil and then rub with a cut clove of garlic. Set aside until ready to serve.

3 Spread the bruschetta with the cheese, roughing it up with a fork, and spoon the tapenade on top. Garnish with sprigs of herbs.

COOK'S TIP
The bruschetta is best grilled over an open flame, if possible. Failing that, a broiler will do, but avoid using a toaster – it gives too even a color and the bruschetta is supposed to look rustic.

WARM AVOCADOS WITH TANGY TOPPING

LIGHTLY BROILED WITH A TASTY TOPPING OF RED ONIONS AND CHEESE, THIS MAKES A DELIGHTFUL ALTERNATIVE TO THE RATHER HUMDRUM AVOCADO VINAIGRETTE.

SERVES FOUR

INGREDIENTS
- 1 small red onion, sliced
- 1 garlic clove, crushed
- 1 tablespoon sunflower oil
- soy sauce
- 2 ripe avocados, halved and pitted
- 2 small tomatoes, sliced
- 1 tablespoon fresh chopped basil, marjoram or parsley
- 2 ounces Lancashire or mozzarella cheese, sliced
- salt and ground black pepper

1 Gently fry the onion and garlic in the oil for about 5 minutes until just softened. Shake in a little soy sauce.

2 Preheat the broiler. Place the avocado halves on the broiler and spoon the onions into the center.

3 Divide the tomato slices and fresh herbs between the four halves and top each one with the cheese.

4 Season well and broil until the cheese melts and starts to brown.

VARIATION
Avocados are wonderful served in other hot dishes too. Try them chopped and tossed with hot pasta or sliced and layered in a lasagne.

LIGHT
LUNCHES
~

MACARONI SOUFFLÉ

*THIS IS GENERALLY A BIG
FAVORITE WITH CHILDREN. IT IS
A LOT LIKE A LIGHT AND FLUFFY
MACARONI AND CHEESE.*

SERVES THREE TO FOUR

INGREDIENTS
    3 ounces elbow macaroni
    melted butter, to coat
    3 tablespoons dried bread crumbs
    4 tablespoons butter
    1 teaspoon ground paprika
    ⅓ cup all-purpose flour
    1¼ cups milk
    6 tablespoons grated Cheddar or
      Gruyère cheese
    4 tablespoons grated Parmesan cheese
    salt and freshly ground black pepper
    3 eggs, separated

1 Boil the macaroni according to
the instructions on the package. Drain
well and set aside. Preheat the oven
to 300°F.

2 Brush the insides of a 1-quart
soufflé dish with melted butter, then coat
evenly with the bread crumbs, shaking
out any excess.

3 Put the butter, paprika, flour and milk
in a saucepan and bring to a boil slowly,
whisking constantly until the mixture is
smooth and thick.

4 Simmer the sauce for a minute, then
remove from the heat and stir in the
cheeses until they melt. Season well and
mix with the macaroni.

5 Beat in the egg yolks. In a clean bowl,
whisk the egg whites until they form soft
peaks and spoon a quarter into the sauce
mixture, beating it gently to loosen it up.

6 Using a large metal spoon, carefully
fold in the rest of the egg whites and
transfer to the prepared soufflé dish.

7 Bake in the center of the oven for
about 40–45 minutes, until the soufflé has
risen and is golden brown. The middle
should wobble very slightly and the soufflé
should be lightly creamy inside.

ADUKI BEAN BURGERS

*ALTHOUGH NOT QUICK TO MAKE,
THESE ARE A DELICIOUS
ALTERNATIVE TO STORE-BOUGHT
BURGERS.*

MAKES 12

INGREDIENTS
    1 cup brown rice
    1 onion, chopped
    2 garlic cloves, crushed
    2 tablespoons sunflower oil
    4 tablespoons butter
    1 small green bell pepper, seeded and
      chopped
    1 carrot, coarsely grated
    1 can (14 ounces) aduki beans, drained
      (or 4 ounces dried weight,
      soaked and cooked)
    1 egg, beaten
    ½ cup grated aged cheese
    1 teaspoon dried thyme
    ½ cup roasted hazelnuts or toasted
      flaked almonds
salt and freshly ground black pepper
whole-wheat flour or cornmeal, for
    coating
oil, for deep-frying

1 Cook the rice according to the instructions on the package, allowing it to slightly overcook so that it is softer. Strain the rice and transfer it to a large bowl.

2 Fry the onion and garlic in the oil and butter together with the green pepper and carrot for about 10 minutes, until the vegetables are softened.

3 Mix this vegetable mixture into the rice, together with the aduki beans, egg, cheese, thyme, nuts or almonds and plenty of seasoning. Chill until firm.

5 Heat ½ inch oil in a large, shallow frying pan and fry the burgers in batches until browned on each side, about 5 minutes total. Remove and drain on paper towels. Eat some burgers freshly cooked, and freeze the rest for later. Serve in buns with salad and relish.

COOK'S TIP
To freeze the burgers, cool them after cooking, then open-freeze them before wrapping and bagging. Use within six weeks. Cook frozen by baking in a preheated, moderately hot oven for 20–25 minutes.

BALTI-STYLE CAULIFLOWER <u>WITH</u> TOMATOES

BALTI IS A TYPE OF MEAT AND VEGETABLE COOKING FROM PAKISTAN AND NORTHERN INDIA. IT CAN REFER BOTH TO THE PAN USED FOR COOKING, WHICH IS LIKE A LITTLE WOK, AND THE SPICES USED. IN THE ABSENCE OF A GENUINE BALTI PAN, USE EITHER A WOK OR A HEAVY FRYING PAN.

SERVES FOUR

INGREDIENTS
- 2 tablespoons vegetable oil
- 1 onion, chopped
- 2 garlic cloves, crushed
- 1 cauliflower, broken into florets
- 1 teaspoon ground coriander
- 1 teaspoon ground cumin
- 1 teaspoon ground fennel seeds
- ½ teaspoon garam masala
- pinch of ground ginger
- ½ teaspoon chili powder
- 4 plum tomatoes, peeled, seeded and quartered
- 6 fluid ounces water
- 6 ounces fresh spinach, roughly chopped
- 1–2 tablespoons lemon juice
- salt and freshly ground black pepper

1 Heat the oil in a balti pan, wok, or large frying pan. Add the onion and garlic and stir-fry for 2–3 minutes over high heat until the onion begins to brown. Add the cauliflower florets and stir-fry for a further 2–3 minutes until the cauliflower is flecked with brown.

2 Add the coriander, cumin, fennel seeds, garam masala, ginger and chili powder and cook over high heat for 1 minute, stirring all the time; then add the tomatoes, water and salt and pepper. Bring to a boil and then reduce the heat, cover and simmer for 5–6 minutes until the cauliflower is just tender.

3 Stir in the chopped spinach, cover and cook for 1 minute until the spinach is tender. Add enough lemon juice to sharpen the flavor and adjust the seasoning to taste.

4 Serve straight from the pan, with an Indian meal or with chicken or meat.

PARSNIP AND CHESTNUT CROQUETTES

THE SWEET NUTTY TASTE OF CHESTNUTS BLENDS PERFECTLY WITH THE SIMILARLY SWEET BUT EARTHY FLAVOR OF PARSNIPS. FRESH CHESTNUTS NEED TO BE PEELED BUT FROZEN CHESTNUTS ARE EASY TO USE AND ARE NEARLY AS GOOD AS FRESH FOR THIS RECIPE.

MAKES TEN TO TWELVE

INGREDIENTS
    1 pound parsnips, cut roughly into
        small pieces
    4 ounces frozen chestnuts
    1 ounce butter
    1 garlic clove, crushed
    1 tablespoon chopped fresh cilantro
    1 egg, beaten
    1½–2 ounces fresh white bread
        crumbs
    vegetable oil, for frying
    salt and freshly ground black pepper
    sprig of cilantro, to garnish

1 Place the parsnips in a saucepan with enough water to cover. Bring to a boil, cover and simmer for 15–20 minutes until completely tender.

2 Place the frozen chestnuts in a pan of water, bring to a boil and simmer for 8–10 minutes until very tender. Drain, place in a bowl and mash roughly.

3 Melt the butter in a small saucepan and cook the garlic for 30 seconds. Drain the parsnips and mash with the garlic butter. Stir in the chestnuts, chopped cilantro and season well.

4 Take about 1 tablespoon of mixture at a time and form into small croquettes, about 3 inches long. Dip each croquette into the beaten egg and then roll in the bread crumbs.

5 Heat a little oil in a frying pan and fry the croquettes for 3–4 minutes until golden, turning frequently so they brown evenly. Drain on paper towels and then serve at once, garnished with cilantro.

SPINACH AND PEPPER PIZZA

MAKES TWO 12-inch PIZZAS

INGREDIENTS

- 1 pound fresh spinach
- 4 tablespoons light cream
- 1 ounce Parmesan cheese, grated
- 1 tablespoon olive oil
- 1 large onion, chopped
- 1 garlic clove, crushed
- ½ green bell pepper, seeded and thinly sliced
- ½ red bell pepper, seeded and thinly sliced
- 6–8 fluid ounces passata sauce or puréed tomatoes
- 2 ounces black olives, pitted and chopped
- 1 tablespoon chopped fresh basil
- 6 ounces mozzarella cheese, grated
- 6 ounces Cheddar cheese, grated
- salt

For the dough

- 1 ounce fresh yeast or 1 tablespoon dried yeast and 1 teaspoon sugar
- 12 ounces unbleached all-purpose flour
- 2 tablespoons olive oil
- 1 teaspoon salt
- about ⅞ cup warm water

1 To make the dough, cream together the fresh yeast and ⅔ cup of the water and set aside until frothy. If using dried yeast, stir the sugar into ⅔ cup water, sprinkle over the yeast and leave until frothy.

2 Place the flour and salt in a large bowl, make a well in the center and pour in the olive oil and yeast mixture. Add the remaining water, mix to make a stiff but pliable dough. Knead on a lightly floured surface for about 10 minutes until smooth and elastic.

3 Shape the dough into a ball and place in a lightly oiled bowl, cover with plastic wrap and leave in a warm place for about 1 hour until it has doubled in size.

4 To prepare the topping, cook the spinach over moderate heat for 4–5 minutes until the leaves have wilted. Strain and press out the excess liquid. Place in a bowl and mix with the cream, Parmesan cheese and salt to taste.

5 Heat the oil in a frying pan and fry the onion and garlic over moderate heat for 3–4 minutes until the onion has slightly softened. Add the peppers and continue cooking until the onion is lightly golden, stirring regularly.

6 Preheat the oven to 425°F. Knead the dough briefly on a lightly floured surface. Divide the dough and roll out into two 12-inch rounds.

7 Spread each base with the passata sauce or puréed tomatoes. Add the onions and peppers and then spread over the spinach mixture. Scatter the olives and basil leaves and sprinkle with the mozzarella and Cheddar cheeses.

8 Bake in the oven for 15–20 minutes, or until the crust is lightly browned and the top is beginning to turn golden. Allow to cool slightly before serving.

ARTICHOKE RÖSTI

SERVES FOUR TO SIX

INGREDIENTS
    1 pound Jerusalem artichokes
    juice of 1 lemon
    1 pound potatoes
    about 2 ounces butter
    salt

1 Peel the Jerusalem artichokes and place in a saucepan of water together with the lemon juice and a pinch of salt. Bring to a boil and cook for about 5 minutes until barely tender.

2 Peel the potatoes and place in a separate pan of salted water. Bring to a boil and cook until barely tender – they will take slightly longer than the artichokes.

3 Drain and cool both the artichokes and potatoes, and then grate them into a bowl. Mix them with your fingers, without breaking them up too much.

4 Melt the butter in a large heavy-based frying pan. Add the artichoke mixture, spreading it out with the back of a spoon. Cook gently for about 10 minutes.

5 Invert the "cake" onto a plate and slide back into the pan. Cook for about 10 minutes until golden. Serve at once.

ARTICHOKE TIMBALES WITH SPINACH SAUCE

SERVES SIX

INGREDIENTS
    2 pounds Jerusalem artichokes
    juice of 1 lemon
    1 ounce butter
    1 tablespoon oil
    1 onion, finely chopped
    1 garlic clove, crushed
    2 ounces fresh white bread crumbs
    1 egg
    4–5 tablespoons vegetable stock
      or milk
    1 tablespoon chopped fresh parsley
    1 teaspoon finely chopped sage
    salt and freshly ground black pepper
For the sauce
    8 ounces fresh spinach, prepared
    ½ ounce butter
    2 shallots, finely chopped
    ⅔ cup light cream
    ¾ cup vegetable stock
    salt and freshly ground black pepper

1 Preheat the oven to 350°F. Grease six ⅔-cup ramekin dishes, and then place a circle of wax paper in the bottom of each.

2 Peel the artichokes and put in a saucepan with the lemon juice and water to cover. Bring to a boil and simmer for about 10 minutes until tender. Drain and mash with the butter.

3 Heat the oil in a small frying pan and fry the onion and garlic until soft. Place in a food processor or blender with the bread crumbs, egg, stock, parsley, sage and seasoning. Process to a smooth purée, add the artichokes and process again briefly using the pulse button.

4 Put the mixture in the prepared dishes. Smooth the tops. Cover with wax paper, place in a roasting pan half-filled with boiling water and bake for 35–40 minutes.

5 To make the sauce, cook the spinach without water, in a large covered saucepan, for 2–3 minutes. Shake the pan occasionally. Strain and press out the excess liquid.

6 Melt the butter in a small saucepan and fry the shallots gently until slightly softened but not browned. Place in a food processor or blender and process to make a smooth purée. Pour back into the pan, add the cream and seasoning, and keep warm over very low heat. Do not allow the mixture to boil.

7 Allow the timbales to stand for a few minutes after cooking and then turn out onto warmed serving plates. Spoon the warm sauce over them and serve.

COOK'S TIP
When puréeing the artichokes in a food processor or blender, use the pulse button and process for a very short time. The mixture will become cloying if it is over-processed.

STUFFED MUSHROOMS

*THIS IS A CLASSIC MUSHROOM DISH, STRONGLY FLAVORED WITH GARLIC. IF YOU PREFER A MORE
SUBTLE GARLIC FLAVOR, BRIEFLY FRY THE GARLIC FIRST.*

SERVES FOUR

INGREDIENTS
  1 pound large flat mushrooms
  butter, for greasing
  3 tablespoons finely chopped fresh
    parsley
  1½–2 ounces fresh white bread crumbs
  2 garlic cloves, minced or very
    finely chopped
  about 5 tablespoons olive oil
  salt and freshly ground black pepper
  sprig Italian parsley, to garnish

1 Preheat the oven to 350°F. Cut off the
mushroom stalks and reserve on one
side.

2 Arrange the mushroom caps in a
buttered shallow dish, gill sides upward.

3 Finely chop the mushroom stalks and
mix with the parsley, bread crumbs,
garlic, 2 tablespoons of the olive oil and
seasoning to taste, and then pile a little
of the mixture into each mushroom.

4 Add the remaining oil to the dish and
cover the mushrooms with buttered wax
paper. Bake for about   15–20 minutes,
removing the paper for the last 5 minutes
to brown the tops. Garnish with a sprig of
Italian parsley.

COOK'S TIP
The cooking time for the mushrooms
depends on their size and thickness. If
they are fairly thin, cook for slightly less
time. They should be tender but not too
soft when cooked. If preferred, the garlic
may be cooked before adding to the
bread crumb mixture. Heat about
1 tablespoon of oil in a frying pan and fry
the garlic very briefly and then stir into
the breadcrumb mixture.

HOT SOUR CHICK-PEAS

THIS DISH, KHATTE CHOLE, IS EATEN AS A SNACK ALL OVER INDIA, SOLD BY ITINERANT STREET VENDORS. THE HEAT OF THE CHILIES IS DAMPENED PARTLY BY THE CILANTRO, WHILE THE LEMON JUICE ADDS A WONDERFUL SOURNESS.

SERVES FOUR

INGREDIENTS

12 ounces chick-peas, soaked overnight
4 tablespoons vegetable oil
2 medium onions, very finely chopped
8 ounces tomatoes, peeled and finely chopped
1 tablespoon ground coriander
1 tablespoon ground cumin
1 teaspoon ground fenugreek
1 teaspoon ground cinnamon
1–2 hot green chilies, seeded and finely sliced
about 1-inch piece fresh ginger, grated
4 tablespoons lemon juice
1 tablespoon chopped fresh cilantro
salt

1 Drain the chick-peas and place them in a large saucepan, cover with water and bring to a boil. Cover and simmer for 1–1¼ hours until tender, making sure the chick-peas do not boil dry. Drain, reserving the cooking liquid.

2 Heat the oil in a large flameproof casserole. Reserve about 2 tablespoons of the chopped onions and fry the remainder in the casserole over moderate heat for 4–5 minutes, stirring frequently, until tinged with brown.

3 Add the tomatoes and continue cooking over moderately low heat for 5–6 minutes until soft. Stir frequently, mashing the tomatoes to a pulp.

4 Stir in the coriander, cumin, fenugreek and cinnamon. Cook for 30 seconds and then add the chick-peas and 12 fluid ounces of the reserved cooking liquid. Season with salt, cover and simmer very gently for about 15–20 minutes, stirring occasionally and adding more cooking liquid if the mixture becomes too dry.

5 Meanwhile, mix the reserved onion with the chili, ginger and lemon juice.

6 Just before serving, stir the onion and chili mixture and the cilantro into the chick-peas, and adjust the seasoning.

HOT BROCCOLI TARTLETS

APART FROM THE UBIQUITOUS QUICHE, VEGETABLE TARTS ARE NOT VERY COMMON IN NORTH AMERICA. HOWEVER, IN FRANCE YOU CAN FIND A WHOLE VARIETY OF SAVORY TARTLETS, FILLED WITH ONIONS, LEEKS, MUSHROOMS AND BROCCOLI.

MAKES EIGHT TO TEN

INGREDIENTS
    1 tablespoon oil
    1 leek, finely sliced
    6 ounces broccoli, broken into florets
    ½ ounce butter
    ½ ounce all-purpose flour
    ⅔ cup milk
    2 ounces Cheddar cheese, grated
    fresh chervil, to garnish
For the pastry
    6 ounces all-purpose flour
    3 ounces butter
    1 egg
    pinch of salt

1 To make the pastry, place the flour and salt in a large bowl and rub in the butter and egg to make a dough. Add a little cold water if necessary, knead lightly, then cover with plastic wrap and leave to rest in the fridge for 1 hour.

2 Preheat the oven to 375°F. Let the dough return to room temperature for 10 minutes and then roll out on a lightly floured surface and line 8–10 deep muffin pans. Prick the bases with a fork and bake in the oven for about 10–15 minutes until the pastry is firm and lightly golden. Increase the oven temperature to 400°F.

3 Heat the oil in a small saucepan and sauté the leek for 4–5 minutes until soft. Add the broccoli, stir-fry for about 1 minute and then add a little water. Cover and steam for 3–4 minutes until the broccoli is just tender.

4 Melt the butter in a separate saucepan, stir in the flour and cook for a minute, stirring all the time. Slowly add the milk and stir to make a smooth sauce. Add half of the cheese and season with salt and pepper.

5 Spoon a little broccoli and leek into each tartlet case and then spoon over the sauce. Sprinkle each tartlet with the remaining cheese and then bake in the oven for about 10 minutes until golden.

6 Serve the tartlets as part of a buffet or as a starter, garnished with chervil.

CAULIFLOWER <u>AND</u> EGG <u>WITH</u> CHEESE

*A QUICK ALL-IN-ONE SAUCE CAN
BE MADE IN MINUTES, WHILE A
SMALL PACKAGE OF SOUP
CROUTONS GIVES THE DISH A
DELICIOUS CRUNCHY TOPPING.*

SERVES FOUR

INGREDIENTS
  1 medium-size cauliflower, in florets
  1 medium onion, sliced
  2 eggs, hard-cooked, peeled and
    chopped
  3 tablespoons whole-wheat flour
  1 teaspoon mild curry powder
  2 tablespoons butter or margarine
  2 cups milk
  ½ teaspoon dried thyme
  salt and freshly ground black pepper
  4 ounces aged cheese, grated
  small package of soup croutons

1 Boil the cauliflower and onion in
enough salted water to cover until they
are just tender. Be careful not to overcook
them. Drain well.

2 Arrange the cauliflower and onion in a
shallow ovenproof dish and top with the
chopped egg.

3 Put the flour, curry powder, butter or
margarine and milk in a saucepan. Bring
slowly to a boil, stirring well, until
thickened and smooth. Stir in the thyme
and seasoning and allow the sauce to
simmer for a minute or two. Remove the
pan from the heat and stir in about three-
quarters of the cheese.

4 Pour the sauce over the cauliflower,
and sprinkle with the croutons and the
remaining cheese. Brown under a hot
broiler until golden and serve. This dish is
delicious with thick crusty bread.

BAKED ZUCCHINI

WHEN VERY SMALL AND VERY FRESH ZUCCHINI ARE USED FOR THIS RECIPE IT IS WONDERFUL, BOTH SIMPLE AND DELICIOUS. THE CREAMY YET TANGY GOAT CHEESE CONTRASTS WELL WITH THE VERY DELICATE FLAVOR OF THE YOUNG ZUCCHINI.

SERVES FOUR

INGREDIENTS

8 small zucchini, about 1 pound total weight

1 tablespoon olive oil, plus extra for greasing

3–4 ounces goat cheese, cut into thin strips

small bunch fresh mint, finely chopped

freshly ground black pepper

1 Preheat the oven to 350°F. Cut out eight rectangles of foil large enough to encase each zucchini and brush each with a little oil.

2 Trim the zucchini and cut a thin slit along the length of each.

3 Insert pieces of goat cheese in the slits. Add a little mint and sprinkle over the olive oil and black pepper.

4 Wrap each zucchini in the foil rectangles, place on a baking sheet and bake for about 25 minutes until tender.

COOK'S TIP
Almost any cheese could be used in this recipe. Mild cheeses, however, such as a mild cheddar or mozzarella, will best allow the flavor of the zucchini to be appreciated.

KITCHIRI

*THIS IS THE INDIAN ORIGINAL
THAT INSPIRED THE CLASSIC
BREAKFAST DISH KNOWN AS
KEDGEREE. MADE WITH BASMATI
RICE AND SMALL, TASTY LENTILS,
THIS WILL MAKE AN AMPLE
SUPPER OR BRUNCH DISH.*

SERVES FOUR

INGREDIENTS

   1 cup Indian masoor
     dal or green lentils
   1 onion, chopped
   1 garlic clove, crushed
   ¼ cup vegetarian ghee or butter
   2 tablespoons sunflower oil
   1¼ cups basmati rice
   2 teaspoons ground coriander
   2 teaspoons cumin seeds
   2 cloves
   3 cardamom pods
   2 bay leaves
   1 stick cinnamon
   4 cups vegetable stock
   2 tablespoons tomato paste
   salt and freshly ground black pepper
   3 tablespoons chopped fresh cilantro or
     parsley, to garnish

1 Cover the dal or lentils with boiling water and soak for 30 minutes. Drain and boil in fresh water for 10 minutes. Drain once more and set aside.

2 Fry the onion and garlic in the ghee or butter and oil in a large saucepan for about 5 minutes.

3 Add the rice, stir well to coat the grains in the ghee or butter and oil, then stir in the spices. Cook gently for a minute or so.

4 Add the lentils, stock, tomato paste and seasoning. Bring to a boil, then cover and simmer for 20 minutes, until the stock is absorbed and the lentils and rice are just soft. Stir in the cilantro or parsley and check the seasoning. Remove the cinnamon stick and bay leaf.

LEEKS IN EGG AND LEMON SAUCE

THE COMBINATION OF EGGS AND LEMON IN SAUCES AND SOUPS IS COMMONLY FOUND IN RECIPES FROM GREECE, TURKEY AND THE MIDDLE EAST. THIS SAUCE HAS A DELICIOUS FRESH TASTE AND BRINGS OUT THE BEST IN THE LEEKS. BE SURE TO USE TENDER BABY LEEKS FOR THIS RECIPE.

SERVES FOUR

INGREDIENTS
    1½ pounds baby leeks
    1 tablespoon cornstarch
    2 teaspoons sugar
    2 egg yolks
    juice of 1½ lemons
    salt

1 Trim the leeks, slit them from top to bottom and rinse very well under cold water to remove any dirt.

2 Place the leeks in a large saucepan, preferably so they lie flat on the bottom, cover with water and add a little salt. Bring to boil, cover and simmer for 4–5 minutes until just tender.

3 Carefully remove the leeks using a slotted spoon, drain well and arrange in a shallow serving dish. Reserve 7 fluid ounces of the cooking liquid.

4 Blend the cornstarch with the cooled cooking liquid and place in a small saucepan. Bring to boil, stirring all the time, and cook over low heat until the sauce thickens slightly. Stir in the sugar and then remove the saucepan from the heat and allow to cool slightly.

5 Beat the egg yolks thoroughly with the lemon juice and stir gradually into the cooled sauce. Cook over very low heat, stirring all the time, until the sauce is fairly thick. Be careful not to overheat the sauce or it may curdle. As soon as the sauce has thickened remove the pan from the heat and continue stirring for a minute. Taste and add salt or sugar as necessary. Cool slightly.

6 Stir the cooled sauce with a wooden spoon. Pour the sauce over the leeks and then cover and chill well for at least 2 hours before serving.

PEANUT BUTTER FINGERS

CHILDREN LOVE THESE CRISPY CROQUETTES. FREEZE SOME READY TO FILL YOUNG TUMMIES!

MAKES 12

INGREDIENTS

    2 pounds potatoes
    1 large onion, chopped
    2 bell peppers, red or green, chopped
    3 carrots, coarsely grated
    3 tablespoons sunflower oil
    2 zucchini, coarsely grated
    4 ounces mushrooms, chopped
    1 tablespoon dried Italian herbs
    ½ cup grated Cheddar cheese
    ½ cup crunchy peanut butter
    salt and freshly ground black pepper
    2 eggs
    ½ cup dried bread crumbs
    3 tablespoons grated Parmesan cheese
    oil, for deep-frying

1 Boil the potatoes until tender, then drain well and mash. Set aside.

2 Fry the onion, peppers and carrot in the oil for about 5 minutes. Add the zucchini and mushrooms and cook for 5 minutes.

3 Mix the potatoes with the dried mixed herbs, grated cheese and peanut butter. Season, allow to cool for 30 minutes, then beat and stir in one of the eggs.

4 Spread the mixture out on a large plate, cool and chill, then divide into 12 portions and shape into fingers. Dip your hands in cold water if the mixture sticks.

5 Beat the second egg in a bowl. Dip the potato fingers into the egg first, then into the crumbs and Parmesan cheese, until coated evenly. Put in fridge to set.

6 Heat oil in a deep-fat frier to 375°F, then fry the fingers in batches for 3 minutes, until golden. Drain well on paper towels. Serve hot.

COOK'S TIP
To reheat, thaw for about 1 hour, then broil or oven bake at 375°F for 15 minutes.

YAM FRITTERS

YAMS HAVE A SLIGHTLY DRIER FLAVOR THAN POTATOES AND ARE PARTICULARLY GOOD WHEN MIXED WITH SPICES AND THEN FRIED. THE FRITTERS CAN ALSO BE MOLDED INTO SMALL BALLS AND DEEP-FRIED. THIS IS A FAVORITE AFRICAN WAY OF SERVING YAMS.

MAKES ABOUT 18–20

INGREDIENTS
    1½ pounds yams
    milk, for mashing
    2 small eggs, beaten
    3 tablespoons chopped tomato flesh
    3 tablespoons finely chopped
      scallions
    1 green chili, seeded and finely sliced
    flour, for shaping
    1½ ounces white bread crumbs
    vegetable oil, for shallow frying
    salt and freshly ground black pepper

1 Peel the yams and cut into chunks. Place in a saucepan of salted water and boil for 20–30 minutes until tender. Drain and mash with a little milk and about 3 tablespoons of the beaten eggs.

2 Add the chopped tomato, scallions, chili and seasoning and stir well.

3 Using floured hands shape the yam and vegetable mixture into round fritters, about 3 inches in diameter.

4 Dip each in the remaining beaten egg and then coat evenly with the bread crumbs. Heat a little oil in a large frying pan and fry the yam fritters for about 4–5 minutes until golden brown. Turn the fritters over once during cooking. Drain well on paper towels and serve.

EDDO, CARROT AND PARSNIP MEDLEY

EDDO (TARO), LIKE YAMS, IS WIDELY EATEN IN AFRICA AND THE CARIBBEAN, OFTEN AS A PURÉE. HERE, IT IS ROASTED AND COMBINED WITH MORE COMMON ROOT VEGETABLES TO MAKE A COLORFUL DISPLAY.

SERVES FOUR TO SIX

INGREDIENTS
    1 pound eddoes or taros
    12 ounces parsnips
    1 pound carrots
    1 ounce butter
    3 tablespoons sunflower oil
For the dressing
    2 tablespoons fresh orange juice
    2 tablespoons brown sugar
    2 teaspoons soft green peppercorns
    salt
    fresh parsley, to garnish

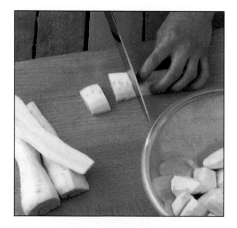

1 Preheat the oven to 400°F. Peel the eddoes and cut into pieces about 2 x ¾ inches, and place in a large bowl.

2 Peel the parsnips, halve lengthwise and remove the inner core if necessary. Cut into the same size pieces as the eddo and add to the bowl. Blanch in boiling water for 2 minutes and then drain. Peel or scrub the carrots, and halve or quarter them according to their size.

3 Place the butter and sunflower oil in a roasting pan and heat in the oven for 3–4 minutes. Add the vegetables, turning them in the oil to coat evenly. Roast in the oven for 30 minutes.

4 Meanwhile, blend the orange juice, sugar and soft green peppercorns in a small bowl. Remove the roasting pan from the oven and allow to cool for a minute or so and then carefully pour the mixture over the vegetables, stirring to coat them all. (If the liquid is poured on immediately, the hot oil will spit.)

5 Return the tin to the oven and cook for a further 20 minutes until the vegetables are crisp and golden. Transfer to a warmed serving plate and sprinkle with salt. Garnish with parsley to serve.

ITALIAN ROAST PEPPERS

SIMPLE AND EFFECTIVE, THIS DISH WILL DELIGHT ANYONE WHO LIKES PEPPERS. IT CAN BE EATEN EITHER AS A STARTER SERVED WITH ITALIAN BREAD, OR AS A LIGHT LUNCH WITH COUSCOUS OR RICE.

SERVES FOUR

INGREDIENTS

    4 small red bell peppers, halved,
      cored and seeded
    2–3 tablespoons capers, chopped
    10–12 black olives, pitted
      and chopped
    2 garlic cloves, finely chopped
    2–3 ounces mozzarella, grated
    1–1½ ounces fresh white bread
      crumbs
    ½ cup white wine
    3 tablespoons olive oil
    1 teaspoon finely chopped fresh mint
    1 teaspoon chopped fresh parsley
    freshly ground black pepper

1 Preheat the oven to 350°F and butter a shallow ovenproof dish. Place the peppers tightly together in the dish and sprinkle over the chopped capers, black olives, garlic, mozzarella and bread crumbs.

2 Pour over the wine and olive oil and then sprinkle with the mint, parsley and freshly ground black pepper.

3 Bake for 30–40 minutes until the topping is crisp and golden brown.

MARROWS WITH GNOCCHI

A SIMPLE WAY WITH MARROW, THIS DISH MAKES AN EXCELLENT ACCOMPANIMENT TO BROILED MEAT BUT IT IS ALSO GOOD WITH A VEGETARIAN DISH, OR SIMPLY SERVED WITH GRILLED TOMATOES.

SERVES FOUR

INGREDIENTS
1 small marrow, cut into
  bite-size chunks
2 ounces butter
14-ounce packet gnocchi
½ garlic clove, crushed
salt and freshly ground black pepper
chopped fresh basil, to garnish

1 Preheat the oven to 350°F and butter a large ovenproof dish. Place the marrow, more or less in a single layer, in the dish. Dot all over with the remaining butter.

2 Place a double piece of buttered wax paper over the top. Cover with an oven-proof plate or lid so that it presses the marrow down, and then place a heavy, ovenproof weight on top of that. (Use a couple of old-fashioned scale weights.)

3 Put in the oven to bake for about 15 minutes, by which time the marrow should just be tender.

4 Cook the gnocchi in a large saucepan of boiling salted water for 2–3 minutes, or according to the instructions on the packet. Drain well.

5 Stir the garlic and gnocchi into the marrow. Season and then place the wax paper over the marrow and return to the oven for 5 minutes (the weights are not necessary).

6 Just before serving, sprinkle the top with a little chopped fresh basil.

SUPPERS

CELERY ROOT AND BLUE CHEESE ROULADE

CELERY ROOT ADDS A DELICATE AND SUBTLE FLAVOR TO THIS ATTRACTIVE DISH. THE SPINACH ROULADE MAKES AN ATTRACTIVE CONTRAST TO THE CREAMY FILLING, BUT YOU COULD USE A PLAIN OR CHEESE ROULADE BASE INSTEAD. BE SURE TO ROLL UP THE ROULADE WHILE IT IS STILL WARM AND PLIABLE.

SERVES SIX

INGREDIENTS
   ½ ounce butter
   8 ounces cooked spinach, drained and
     chopped
   ⅔ cup light cream
   4 large eggs, separated
   ½ ounce Parmesan cheese, grated
   pinch of nutmeg
   salt and freshly ground black pepper
For the filling
   8 ounces celery root
   lemon juice
   3 ounces blue cheese
   4 ounces ricotta cheese
   freshly ground black pepper

1 Preheat the oven to 400°F and line a 13 x 9-inch jelly roll tin with non-stick baking parchment.

2 Melt the butter in a saucepan and add the spinach. Cook gently until all the liquid has evaporated, stirring frequently. Remove the pan from the heat and stir in the cream, egg yolks, Parmesan cheese, nutmeg and seasoning.

3 Whisk the egg whites until stiff, fold them gently into the spinach mixture and then spoon into the prepared pan. Spread the mixture evenly and use a metal spatula to smooth the surface.

4 Bake in the oven for 10–15 minutes until the roulade is firm to the touch and lightly golden on top. Carefully turn out onto a sheet of wax paper and peel away the lining paper. Roll it up with the paper inside and leave to cool slightly.

5 To make the filling, peel and grate the celery root into a bowl and sprinkle well with lemon juice. Blend the blue cheese and ricotta cheese together and mix with the celery root and a little black pepper.

6 Unroll the roulade, spread with the filling and roll up again. Serve at once or wrap loosely and chill.

LOOFAH AND EGGPLANT RATATOUILLE

LOOFAHS HAVE A SIMILAR FLAVOR TO ZUCCHINI AND CONSEQUENTLY TASTE EXCELLENT WITH EGGPLANT AND TOMATOES. THE CILANTRO ADDS AN EXTRA EXOTIC TOUCH.

SERVES FOUR

INGREDIENTS

1 large or 2 medium eggplants
1 pound young loofahs or
 sponge gourds
1 large red bell pepper, cut into
 large chunks
8 ounces cherry tomatoes
8 ounces shallots, peeled
2 teaspoons ground coriander
4 tablespoons olive oil
2 garlic cloves, finely chopped
a few cilantro leaves
salt and freshly ground black pepper

1 Cut the eggplants into thick chunks and sprinkle the pieces with salt. Set aside in a colander for about 45 minutes and then rinse well under cold running water and pat dry.

2 Preheat the oven to 425°F. Slice the loofahs into ¾-inch pieces. Place the eggplant, loofah and pepper pieces, together with the tomatoes and shallots in a roasting pan which is large enough to take all the vegetables in a single layer.

3 Sprinkle with the ground coriander and olive oil and then scatter the chopped garlic and cilantro leaves on top. Season to taste.

4 Roast for about 25 minutes, stirring the vegetables occasionally, until the loofah is golden brown and the peppers are beginning to char at the edges.

RADICCHIO PIZZA

THIS UNUSUAL PIZZA TOPPING CONSISTS OF CHOPPED RADICCHIO WITH LEEKS, TOMATOES AND PARMESAN AND MOZZARELLA CHEESES. THE BASE IS A SCONE DOUGH, MAKING THIS A QUICK AND EASY SUPPER DISH TO PREPARE. SERVE WITH A CRISP GREEN SALAD.

SERVES TWO

INGREDIENTS
14-ounce can chopped tomatoes
2 garlic cloves, crushed
pinch of dried basil
1½ tablespoons olive oil, plus extra
    for dipping
2 leeks, sliced
3½ ounces radicchio, roughly chopped
¾ ounces Parmesan cheese, grated
4 ounces mozzarella cheese, sliced
10–12 black olives, pitted
basil leaves, to garnish
salt and freshly ground black pepper
For the dough
8 ounces self-rising flour
½ teaspoon salt
2 ounces butter or margarine
about ½ cup milk

1 Preheat the oven to 425°F and grease a baking sheet. Mix the flour and salt in a bowl, rub in the butter or margarine and gradually stir in the milk and water and mix to a soft dough.

2 Roll the dough out on a lightly floured surface to make a 10–11-inch round. Place on the baking sheet.

3 Purée the tomatoes and then pour into a small saucepan. Stir in one of the crushed garlic cloves, together with the dried basil and seasoning, and simmer over moderate heat until the mixture is thick and reduced by about half.

4 Heat the olive oil in a large frying pan and fry the leeks and remaining garlic for 4–5 minutes until slightly softened. Add the radicchio and cook, stirring continuously for a few minutes, and then cover and simmer gently for about 5–10 minutes. Stir in the Parmesan cheese and season with salt and pepper.

5 Cover the dough base with the tomato mixture and then spoon the leek and radicchio mixture on top. Arrange the mozzarella slices on top and scatter over the black olives. Dip a few basil leaves in olive oil, arrange on top and then bake the pizza for 15–20 minutes until the scone base and top are golden brown.

TAGLIATELLE FUNGI

THE MUSHROOM SAUCE IS QUICK TO MAKE AND THE PASTA COOKS VERY QUICKLY; BOTH NEED TO BE COOKED AS NEAR TO SERVING AS POSSIBLE SO CAREFUL COORDINATION IS REQUIRED. PUT THE PASTA IN TO COOK WHEN THE MASCARPONE CHEESE IS ADDED TO THE SAUCE.

SERVES FOUR (as a snack or starter)

INGREDIENTS
    about 2 ounces butter
    8–12 ounces chanterelles or other
        wild mushrooms
    1 tablespoon all-purpose flour
    ⅔ cup milk
    6 tablespoons crème fraiche or sour
        cream
    1 tablespoon chopped fresh parsley
    10 ounces fresh tagliatelle
    olive oil
    salt and freshly ground black pepper

3 Add the crème fraiche or sour cream, parsley, mushrooms and seasoning and stir well. Cook gently to heat through and then keep warm while cooking the pasta.

4 Cook the pasta in a large saucepan of boiling water for 4–5 minutes (or according to the instructions on the packet). Drain well, toss in a little olive oil and then turn onto a warmed serving plate. Pour the mushroom sauce over and serve immediately.

COOK'S TIP
Chanterelles are a little tricky to wash, as they are so delicate. However, since these are woodland mushrooms, it's important to clean them thoroughly. Hold each one by the stalk and let cold water run under the gills to dislodge hidden dirt. Shake gently to dry.

1 Melt 1½ ounces of the butter in a frying pan and fry the mushrooms for about 2–3 minutes over low heat until the juices begin to run, then increase the heat and cook until the liquid has almost evaporated. Transfer the mushrooms to a bowl using a slotted spoon.

2 Stir in the flour, adding a little more butter if necessary, and cook for about 1 minute, and then gradually stir in the milk to make a smooth sauce.

TANGY FRICASSEE

VEGETABLES IN A LIGHT TANGY SAUCE COVERED WITH A CRISPY CRUMB TOPPING MAKE A SIMPLE AND EASY MAIN COURSE TO SERVE WITH CRUSTY BREAD AND SALAD.

SERVES FOUR

INGREDIENTS

4 zucchini, sliced
4 ounces green beans, sliced
4 large tomatoes, peeled and sliced
1 onion, sliced
4 tablespoons butter or sunflower
  margarine
⅓ cup all-purpose flour
2 teaspoons coarse-grained mustard
2 cups milk
⅔ cup plain yogurt
1 teaspoon dried thyme
4 ounces aged cheese, grated
salt and freshly ground black pepper
¼ cup fresh whole-wheat bread crumbs
  tossed with
1 tablespoon sunflower oil

1 Blanch the zucchini and beans in a small amount of boiling water for just 5 minutes, then drain and arrange in a shallow ovenproof dish. Arrange all but three slices of tomato on top. Put the onion in a saucepan with the butter or margarine and fry gently for 5 minutes.

2 Stir in the flour and mustard, cook for a minute, then add the milk gradually until the sauce has thickened. Simmer for another 2 minutes.

3 Remove the pan from the heat and add the yogurt, thyme and cheese, stirring until melted. Season to taste. Reheat gently if you wish, but do not allow the sauce to boil or it will curdle.

4 Pour the sauce over the vegetables and scatter the bread crumbs on top. Brown under a preheated broiler until golden and crisp, taking care not to let the bread crumbs burn. Garnish with the reserved tomato slices if desired.

WILD MUSHROOMS IN BRIOCHE

SERVES FOUR

INGREDIENTS
   4 small brioches
   olive oil, for glazing
   4 teaspoons lemon juice
   sprigs of parsley, to garnish
For the mushroom filling
   1 ounce butter
   2 shallots
   1 garlic clove, crushed
   6–8 ounces assorted wild mushrooms,
      halved if large
   3 tablespoons white wine
   3 tablespoons double cream
   1 teaspoon chopped fresh basil
   1 teaspoon chopped fresh parsley
   salt and freshly ground black pepper

1 Preheat the oven to 350°F. Using a serrated or grapefruit knife, cut a circle out of the top of the brioche and reserve. Scoop out the bread inside to make a small cavity.

2 Place the brioches and the tops on a baking sheet and brush inside and out with olive oil. Bake for 7–10 minutes until golden and crisp. Squeeze 1 teaspoon of lemon juice inside each brioche

3 To make the filling, melt the butter in a frying pan and fry the shallots and garlic for 2–3 minutes until softened.

4 Add the mushrooms and cook gently for about 4–5 minutes, stirring.

5 When the juices begin to run, reduce the heat and continue cooking for about 3–4 minutes, stirring occasionally, until the pan is fairly dry.

6 Stir in the wine. Cook for a few more minutes and then stir in the cream, basil, parsley and seasoning to taste.

7 Pile the mushroom mixture into the brioche shells and return to the oven and reheat for about 5–6 minutes. Serve as a starter, garnished with a sprig of parsley.

WILD MUSHROOMS WITH PANCAKES

SERVES SIX (as a starter)

INGREDIENTS
   8–10 ounces assorted wild
      mushrooms
   2 ounces butter
   1–2 garlic cloves
   splash of brandy (optional)
   freshly ground black pepper
   sour cream, to serve
For the pancakes
   4 ounces self-rising flour
   ¾ ounce buckwheat flour
   ½ teaspoon baking powder
   pinch of salt
   2 eggs
   about 1 cup milk
   oil, for frying

1 To make the pancakes, mix together the flours, baking powder and salt in a large bowl or food processor. Add the eggs and milk and beat or process to make a smooth batter, about the consistency of light cream.

2 Grease a large griddle or frying pan with a little oil and when hot, pour small amounts of batter (about 1–2 tablespoons per pancake) onto the griddle, well spaced apart.

3 Fry for a few minutes until bubbles begin to appear on the surface and the underside is golden, and then flip over. Cook for about 1 minute until golden. Keep warm, wrapped in a clean dish towel. (Makes about 18–20 pancakes.)

4 If the mushrooms are large, cut them in half. Melt the butter in a frying pan and add the garlic and mushrooms. Fry over moderate heat for a few minutes until the juices begin to run and then increase the heat and cook, stirring frequently, until nearly all the juices have evaporated. Stir in the brandy, if using, and season with a little black pepper.

5 Arrange the warm pancakes on a serving plate and spoon over a little sour cream. Top with the hot mushrooms and serve immediately.

COOK'S TIP
This makes a delicious and elegant starter for a dinner party. Alternatively, make cocktail-size pancakes and serve as part of a buffet supper.

KOHLRABI STUFFED WITH PEPPERS

IF YOU HAVEN'T SAMPLED KOHLRABI, OR HAVE ONLY EATEN IT IN STEWS WHERE ITS FLAVOR IS LOST, THIS DISH IS RECOMMENDED. THE SLIGHTLY SHARP FLAVOR OF THE PEPPERS IS AN EXCELLENT FOIL TO THE MORE EARTHY FLAVOR OF THE KOHLRABI.

SERVES FOUR

INGREDIENTS

4 small kohlrabi, about 6–8 ounces each

about 1⅔ cups hot vegetable stock

1 tablespoon olive or sunflower oil

1 onion, chopped

1 small red bell pepper, seeded and sliced

1 small green bell pepper, seeded and sliced

salt and freshly ground black pepper

flat leaf parsley, to garnish (optional)

1 Preheat the oven to 350°F. Trim and remove the ends of the kohlrabi, and arrange in the bottom of a medium-size ovenproof dish.

2 Pour over the stock to come about halfway up the vegetables. Cover and braise in the oven for about 30 minutes until tender. Transfer to a plate and allow to cool, reserving the stock.

3 Heat the oil in a frying pan and fry the onion for 3–4 minutes over low heat, stirring occasionally. Add the peppers and cook for a further 2–3 minutes, until the onion is lightly browned.

4 Add the reserved vegetable stock, and a little seasoning and simmer, uncovered, over moderate heat until the stock has almost evaporated.

5 Scoop out the flesh from the kohlrabis and roughly chop. Stir the flesh into the onion and pepper mixture, taste and adjust the seasoning. Arrange the shells in a shallow ovenproof dish.

6 Spoon the filling into the kohlrabi shells. Place in the oven for 5–10 minutes to heat through and then serve, garnished with flat leaf parsley, if liked.

LEEK SOUFFLÉ

Some people think of a soufflé as a dinner party dish, and a rather tricky one at that. However, others frequently serve them for family meals because they are quick and easy to make, and prove to be very popular and satisfying.

SERVES TWO TO THREE

INGREDIENTS

   1 tablespoon sunflower oil
   1½ ounces butter
   2 leeks, thinly sliced
   about 1¼ cups milk
   1 ounce all-purpose flour
   4 eggs, separated
   3 ounces Gruyère or Emmenthal
     cheese, grated
   salt and freshly ground black pepper

1 Preheat the oven to 350ºF and butter a large soufflé dish. Heat the oil and ½ ounce of the butter in a small saucepan or flameproof casserole and fry the leeks over low heat for 4–5 minutes until soft but not brown, stirring occasionally.

2 Stir in the milk and bring to boil. Cover and simmer for 4–5 minutes until the leeks are tender. Put the liquid through a strainer into a measuring jug.

3 Melt the remaining butter in a saucepan, stir in the flour and cook for 1 minute. Remove pan from the heat. Make up the reserved liquid with milk to 1¼ cups. Gradually stir the milk into the pan to make a smooth sauce. Return to the heat and bring to a boil, stirring. When thickened, remove from the heat. Cool slightly and then beat in the egg yolks, cheese and the leeks.

4 Whisk the egg whites until stiff and, using a large metal spoon, fold into the leek and egg mixture. Pour into the prepared soufflé dish and bake in the oven for about 30 minutes until golden and puffy. Serve immediately.

SPINACH RAVIOLI

HOME-MADE RAVIOLI IS TIME-CONSUMING, YET IT IS WORTH THE EFFORT AS EVEN THE BEST SHOP-BOUGHT PASTA NEVER TASTES QUITE AS FRESH. TO COMPLEMENT THIS EFFORT, MAKE THE FILLING EXACTLY TO YOUR LIKING, TASTING IT FOR THE RIGHT BALANCE OF SPINACH AND CHEESE.

SERVES FOUR

INGREDIENTS
8 ounces fresh spinach
1½ ounces butter
1 small onion, finely chopped
1 ounce Parmesan cheese, grated
1½ ounces Dolcellate cheese,
   crumbled
1 tablespoon chopped fresh parsley
salt and freshly ground black pepper
For the pasta dough
12 ounces unbleached all-purpose
   flour
¾ teaspoon salt
2 eggs
1 tablespoon olive oil
shavings of Parmesan cheese, to serve

1 To make the pasta dough, mix together the flour and salt in a large bowl or food processor. Add the eggs, olive oil and about 3 tablespoons of cold water or enough to make a pliable dough. If working by hand, mix the ingredients together and then knead the dough for about 15 minutes until very smooth. Or, process for about 1½ minutes in a food processor. Place the dough in a plastic bag and chill for at least 1 hour (or overnight if more convenient).

2 Cook the spinach in a large, covered saucepan for 3–4 minutes, until the leaves have wilted. Strain and press out the excess liquid. Set aside to cool a little and then chop finely.

3 Melt half the butter in a small saucepan and fry the onion over low heat for about 5–6 minutes until soft. Place in a bowl with the chopped spinach, the Parmesan and Dolcellate cheeses, and seasoning. Mix well.

4 Grease a ravioli sheet. Roll out half or a quarter of the pasta dough to a thickness of about ⅛ inch. Lay the dough over the ravioli sheet, pressing it well into each of the squares.

5 Spoon a little spinach mixture into each cavity, then roll out a second piece of dough and lay it on top. Press a rolling pin evenly over the top of the sheet to seal the edges and then cut the ravioli into squares using a pastry cutter.

6 Place the ravioli in a large saucepan of boiling water and simmer for about 4–5 minutes until cooked through but *al dente*. Drain well and then toss with the remaining butter and the parsley.

7 Divide between four serving plates and serve scattered with shavings of Parmesan cheese.

COOK'S TIP
For a small ravioli sheet of 32 holes, divide the dough into quarters. Roll the dough out until it covers the sheet comfortably – it takes some time but the pasta needs to be thin otherwise the ravioli will be too stodgy. For a large ravioli sheet of 64 holes, divide the dough in half.

SPINACH AND CANNELLINI BEANS

THIS HEARTY DISH CAN BE MADE WITH ALMOST ANY DRIED BEAN OR PEA, SUCH AS BLACK-EYED PEAS, HARICOTS OR CHICK-PEAS. IT IS A GOOD DISH TO SERVE ON A COLD EVENING.

SERVES FOUR

INGREDIENTS
  8 ounces cannellini beans,
    soaked overnight
  3 tablespoons olive oil
  1 slice white bread
  1 onion, chopped
  3–4 tomatoes, peeled and chopped
  a good pinch of paprika
  1 pound spinach
  1 garlic clove, halved
  salt and freshly ground black pepper

1 Drain the beans, place in a saucepan and cover with water. Bring to a boil and boil rapidly for 10 minutes. Cover and simmer for about 1 hour until the beans are tender. Drain.

2 Heat 2 tablespoons of the oil in a frying pan and fry the bread until golden brown. Transfer to a plate.

3 Fry the onion in the remaining oil over low heat until soft but not brown, then add the tomatoes and continue cooking over low heat.

4 Heat the remaining oil in a large pan, stir in the paprika and then add the spinach. Cover and cook for a few minutes until the spinach has wilted.

5 Add the onion and tomato mixture to the spinach, mix well and stir in the cannellini beans. Place the garlic and fried bread in a food processor and process until smooth. Stir into the spinach and bean mixture. Add ⅔ cup cold water and then cover and simmer gently for 20–30 minutes, adding more water if necessary.

CORN AND CHEESE PASTIES

THESE TASTY PASTIES ARE REALLY SIMPLE TO MAKE AND IRRESISTIBLE — WHY NOT MAKE DOUBLE THE AMOUNT, AS THEY'LL GO LIKE HOTCAKES.

MAKES 18–20

INGREDIENTS

9 ounces corn
4 ounces feta cheese
1 egg, beaten
2 tablespoons heavy or whipping cream
½ ounce Parmesan cheese, grated
3 scallions, chopped
8–10 small sheets filo pastry
4 ounces butter, melted
freshly ground black pepper

1 Preheat the oven to 375°F and butter two muffin pans.

2 If using fresh corn, strip the kernels from the cob using a sharp knife and simmer in a little salted water for 3–5 minutes until tender. For canned corn, drain and rinse well under cold running water.

3 Crumble the feta cheese into a bowl and stir in the corn. Add the egg, cream, Parmesan cheese, scallions and ground black pepper, and stir well.

4 Take one sheet of pastry and cut it in half to make a square. (Keep the remaining pastry covered with a damp cloth to prevent it drying out.) Brush with melted butter and then fold into four, to make a smaller square (about 3 inches).

5 Place a heaped teaspoon of mixture in the center of each pastry square and then squeeze the pastry around the filling to make a "money bag" casing.

6 Continue making pasties until all the mixture is used up. Brush the outside of each "bag" with any remaining butter and then bake in the oven for about 20–25 minutes until golden. Serve hot.

CASSAVA AND VEGETABLE KEBABS

THIS IS AN ATTRACTIVE AND DELICIOUS ASSORTMENT OF AFRICAN VEGETABLES, MARINATED IN A SPICY GARLIC SAUCE. IF CASSAVA IS UNAVAILABLE, USE SWEET POTATO OR YAM INSTEAD.

SERVES FOUR

INGREDIENTS
- 6 ounces cassava
- 1 onion, cut into wedges
- 1 eggplant, cut into bite-size pieces
- 1 zucchini, sliced
- 1 ripe plantain, sliced
- 1 red pepper or ½ red bell pepper,
  ½ green bell pepper, sliced
- 16 cherry tomatoes

For the marinade
- 4 tablespoons lemon juice
- 4 tablespoons olive oil
- 3–4 tablespoons soy sauce
- 1 tablespoon tomato paste
- 1 green chili, seeded and finely
  chopped
- ½ onion, grated
- 2 garlic cloves, crushed
- 1 teaspoon mixed spice
- pinch dried thyme
- rice or couscous, to serve

1 Peel the cassava and cut into bite-size pieces. Place in a bowl, cover with boiling water and leave to blanch for 5 minutes. Drain well.

2 Place all the vegetables, including the cassava, in a large bowl.

3 Blend together all the marinade ingredients and pour over the prepared vegetables. Set aside for 1–2 hours.

4 Preheat the broiler and thread all the vegetables and cherry tomatoes onto eight skewers.

5 Broil the vegetables under low heat for about 15 minutes until tender and browned, turning frequently and basting occasionally with the marinade.

6 Meanwhile, pour the remaining marinade into a small saucepan and simmer for 10 minutes until slightly reduced.

7 Arrange the vegetable kebabs on a serving plate and strain the sauce into a small jug. Serve with rice or couscous.

TURNIP AND CHICKPEA COBBLER

A GOOD MIDWEEK MEAL.

<u>SERVES FOUR TO SIX</u>

INGREDIENTS

   1 onion, sliced
   2 carrots, chopped
   3 medium size turnips, chopped
   1 small sweet potato or rutabaga, chopped
   2 celery stalks, sliced thinly
   3 tablespoons sunflower oil
   ½ teaspoon ground coriander
   ½ teaspoon dried Italian herbs
   1 can (14 ounces) tomatoes, chopped
   1 can (14 ounces) chickpeas
   1 vegetable bouillon cube
   salt and freshly ground black pepper
For the topping
   2 cups self-rising flour
   1 teaspoon baking powder
   4 tablespoons margarine
   3 tablespoons sunflower seeds
   2 tablespoons grated Parmesan cheese
   ⅔ cup milk

1 Fry all the vegetables in the oil for about 10 minutes, until they are soft. Add the coriander, herbs, tomatoes, chickpeas with their liquid and bouillon cube. Season well and simmer for 20 minutes.

2 Pour the vegetables into a shallow casserole dish while you make the topping. Preheat the oven to 375°F.

3 Mix together the flour and baking powder, then rub in the margarine until the mixture resembles fine crumbs. Stir in the seeds and Parmesan cheese. Add the milk and mix to a firm dough.

4 Lightly roll out the dough to a thickness of ½ inch and stamp out star shapes or circles, or simply cut it into small squares.

5 Place the shapes on top of the vegetable mixture and brush with a little extra milk. Bake for 12–15 minutes, until risen and golden brown. Serve hot with green, leafy vegetables.

BAKED LEEKS WITH CHEESE AND YOGURT TOPPING

LIKE ALL VEGETABLES, THE FRESHER LEEKS ARE, THE BETTER THEIR FLAVOR, AND THE FRESHEST LEEKS AVAILABLE SHOULD BE USED FOR THIS DISH. SMALL, YOUNG LEEKS ARE AROUND AT THE BEGINNING OF THE SEASON AND ARE PERFECT TO USE HERE.

SERVES FOUR

INGREDIENTS
  8 small leeks, about 1½ pounds
  2 small eggs or 1 large one, beaten
  5 ounces fresh goat cheese
  ⅓ cup plain yogurt
  2 ounces Parmesan cheese, grated
  1 ounce fresh white or brown bread
    crumbs
salt and freshly ground black pepper

1 Preheat the oven to 350°F and butter a shallow ovenproof dish. Trim the leeks, cut a slit from top to bottom and rinse well under cold water.

2 Place the leeks in a saucepan of water, bring to the boil and simmer gently for 6–8 minutes until just tender. Remove and drain well using a slotted spoon, and arrange in the prepared dish.

3 Beat the eggs with the goat cheese, yogurt and half the Parmesan cheese, and season well with salt and pepper.

4 Pour the cheese and yogurt mixture over the leeks. Mix the bread crumbs and remaining Parmesan cheese together and sprinkle over the sauce. Bake in the oven for 35–40 minutes until the top is crisp and golden brown.

CAULIFLOWER <u>AND</u> MUSHROOM GOUGÈRE

THIS IS AN ALL-ROUND FAVORITE VEGETARIAN DISH. WHEN COOKING THIS DISH FOR MEAT LOVERS, CHOPPED ROAST HAM OR FRIED BACON CAN BE ADDED.

SERVES FOUR TO SIX

INGREDIENTS
   1¼ cups water
   4 ounces butter or margarine
   5 ounces all-purpose flour
   4 eggs
   4 ounces Gruyère or Cheddar cheese,
      finely diced
   1 teaspoon French mustard
   salt and freshly ground black pepper
For the filling
   14-ounce can tomatoes
   1 tablespoon sunflower oil
   ½ ounce butter or margarine
   1 onion, chopped
   4 ounces white mushrooms, halved if
      large
   1 small cauliflower, broken into
      small florets
   sprig of thyme
   salt and freshly ground black pepper

1 Preheat the oven to 400°F and butter a large oval ovenproof dish. Place the water and butter together in a large saucepan and heat until the butter has melted. Remove from the heat and add all the flour at once. Beat well with a wooden spoon for about 30 seconds until smooth. Allow to cool slightly.

2 Beat in the eggs, one at a time, and continue beating until the mixture is thick and glossy. Stir in the cheese and mustard and season with salt and pepper. Spread the mixture around the sides of the ovenproof dish, leaving a hollow in the center for the filling.

3 To make the filling, purée the tomatoes in a blender or food processor and then pour into a measuring jug. Add enough water to make up to 1¼ cups of liquid.

4 Heat the oil and butter in a flameproof casserole and fry the onion for about 3–4 minutes until softened but not browned. Add the mushrooms and cook for 2–3 minutes until they begin to be flecked with brown. Add the cauliflower florets and stir-fry for 1 minute.

5 Add the tomato liquid, thyme and seasoning. Cook, uncovered, over low heat for about 5 minutes until the cauliflower is only just tender.

6 Spoon the mixture into the hollow in the ovenproof dish, adding all the liquid. Bake in the oven for about 35–40 minutes, until the outer pastry is well risen and golden brown.

COOK'S TIP
For a variation, ham or bacon can be added. Use about 4–5 ounces thickly sliced roast ham and add to the sauce at the end of step 5.

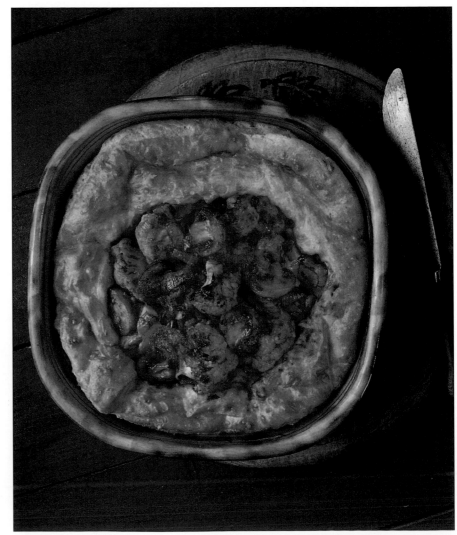

SPINACH IN FILO WITH THREE CHEESES

A GOOD CHOICE TO SERVE WHEN VEGETARIANS AND MEAT EATERS ARE GATHERED FOR A MEAL, AS WHATEVER THEIR PREFERENCE, EVERYONE SEEMS PARTIAL TO THIS TASTY DISH.

SERVES FOUR

INGREDIENTS
   1 pound spinach
   1 tablespoon sunflower oil
   ½ ounce butter
   1 small onion, finely chopped
   6 ounces ricotta cheese
   4 ounces feta cheese, cut into
     small cubes
   3 ounces Gruyère or Emmenthal
     cheese, grated
   1 tablespoon fresh chopped chervil
   1 teaspoon fresh chopped marjoram
   salt and freshly ground black pepper
   5 large or 10 small sheets filo pastry
   1½–2 ounces butter, melted

1 Preheat the oven to 375°F. Cook the spinach in a large saucepan over moderate heat for 3–4 minutes until the leaves have wilted, shaking the saucepan occasionally. Strain and press out the excess liquid.

2 Heat the oil and butter in a saucepan and fry the onion for 3–4 minutes until softened. Remove from the heat and add half of the spinach. Combine using a metal spoon, breaking up the spinach.

3 Add the ricotta cheese and stir until evenly combined. Stir in the remaining spinach, again chopping it into the mixture with a metal spoon. Fold in the feta and Gruyère or Emmenthal cheeses, chervil, marjoram and seasoning.

4 Lay a sheet of filo pastry measuring about 12 inches square on a work surface. (If you have small filo sheets, lay them side by side, overlapping by about 1 inch in the middle.) Brush with melted butter and cover with a second sheet; brush this with butter and build up five layers of pastry in this way.

5 Spread the filling over the pastry, leaving a 1-inch border. Fold the two shorter sides inward and then roll up.

6 Place the roll, seam side down, on a greased baking sheet and brush with the remaining butter. Bake in the oven for about 30 minutes until golden brown.

EGGS FLAMENCO

A VARIATION OF THE POPULAR BASQUE DISH PIPERADE, THE EGGS ARE COOKED WHOLE INSTEAD OF BEATING THEM BEFORE ADDING TO THE PEPPER MIXTURE. THE RECIPE IS KNOWN AS CHAKCHOUKA IN NORTH AFRICA AND MAKES A GOOD LUNCH OR SUPPER DISH.

SERVES FOUR

INGREDIENTS

2 red bell peppers, seeded
1 green bell pepper, seeded
2 tablespoons olive oil
1 large onion, finely sliced
2 garlic cloves, crushed
5–6 tomatoes, peeled and chopped
½ cup puréed canned tomatoes or tomato juice
good pinch of dried basil
4 eggs
8 teaspoons light cream
pinch of cayenne pepper (optional)
salt and freshly ground black pepper

1 Preheat the oven to 350°F. Thinly slice the red and green peppers. Heat the olive oil in a large frying pan. Fry the onion and garlic gently for about 5 minutes, stirring, until softened.

2 Add the peppers to the onions and fry for 10 minutes. Stir in the tomatoes and tomato purée or juice, the basil and seasoning. Cook gently for a further 10 minutes until the peppers are soft.

3 Spoon the mixture into four ovenproof dishes, preferably earthenware. Make a hole in the centre and break an egg into each. Spoon 2 teaspoons cream over the yolk of each egg and sprinkle with a little black pepper or cayenne, as preferred.

4 Bake in the oven for 12–15 minutes until the white of the egg is lightly set. Serve at once with chunks of crusty warm Italian bread.

BAKED MARROW IN PARSLEY SAUCE

THIS IS A REALLY GLORIOUS WAY WITH A SIMPLE AND MODEST VEGETABLE. TRY TO FIND A SMALL, FIRM AND UNBLEMISHED MARROW FOR THIS RECIPE, AS THE FLAVOR WILL BE SWEET, FRESH AND DELICATE.

SERVES FOUR

INGREDIENTS
1 small young marrow, about 2 pounds
2 tablespoons olive oil
½ ounce butter
1 onion, chopped
1 tablespoon all-purpose flour
1¼ cups milk and light cream mixed
2 tablespoons chopped fresh parsley
salt and freshly ground black pepper

1 Preheat the oven to 350°F and cut the marrow into pieces measuring about 2 x 1 inches.

2 Heat the oil and butter in a flameproof casserole and fry the onion over a gentle heat until very soft.

3 Add the marrow and sauté for 1–2 minutes and then stir in the flour. Cook for a few minutes and then stir in the milk and cream mixture.

4 Add the parsley and seasoning, stir well and then cover and cook in the oven for 30–35 minutes. If liked, remove the lid for the final 5 minutes of cooking to brown the top. Alternately, serve the marrow in its rich pale sauce.

COOK'S TIP
Chopped fresh basil or a mixture of basil and chervil also tastes good in this dish.

FESTIVE JALOUSIE

AN EXCELLENT PIE TO SERVE DURING THE HOLIDAY PERIOD. USE CHINESE DRIED CHESTNUTS, SOAKED AND COOKED, INSTEAD OF FRESH ONES.

SERVES SIX

INGREDIENTS

    1 pound puff pastry, thawed if frozen
    1 pound Brussels sprouts, trimmed
    16 whole chestnuts, peeled if fresh
    1 large red bell pepper, sliced
    1 large onion, sliced
    3 tablespoons sunflower oil
    1 egg yolk, beaten with 1 tablespoon
      water
For the sauce
    scant ½ cup all-purpose flour
    3 tablespoons butter
    ½ pint milk
    3 ounces Cheddar cheese, grated
    2 tablespoons dry sherry
    generous pinch of dried sage
    salt and freshly ground black pepper
    3 tablespoons chopped fresh parsley

2 Blanch the Brussels sprouts for 4 minutes in 1 cup boiling water, then drain, reserving the water. Refresh the sprouts under cold running water.

3 Cut each chestnut in half. Lightly fry the red pepper and onion in the oil for 5 minutes. Set aside.

6 Fit the larger piece of pastry into a pie dish and layer the Brussels sprouts, chestnuts, peppers and onions on top. Drizzle with the sauce, making sure it seeps through to wet the vegetables.

7 Brush the pastry edges with beaten egg yolk and fit the second pastry sheet on top, pressing the edges well to seal them.

8 Crimp the edges, then mark the center. Glaze well with egg yolk. Set aside to rest somewhere cool while you preheat the oven to 400°F. Bake for 30–40 minutes, until golden brown and crisp.

1 Roll out the pastry to make two large rectangles, roughly the size of your dish. The pastry should be about ¼ inch thick and one rectangle should be slightly larger than the other. Set the pastry aside in the refrigerator.

4 Make the sauce by beating the flour, butter and milk together over medium heat. Beat the sauce continuously, bringing it to a boil and stirring until it is thickened and smooth.

5 Stir in the reserved sprout water and the cheese, sherry, sage and seasoning. Simmer for 3 minutes to reduce and stir in the parsley.

CELERY ROOT GRATIN

Although celery root has a rather unattractive appearance with its hard, knobbly skin, it is a vegetable that has a very delicious sweet and nutty flavor. This is accentuated in this dish by the addition of the sweet yet nutty Emmental cheese.

SERVES FOUR

INGREDIENTS

    1 pound celery root
    juice of ½ lemon
    1 ounce butter
    1 small onion, finely chopped
    2 tablespoons all-purpose flour
    1¼ cups milk
    1 ounce Emmental cheese, grated
    1 tablespoon capers
    salt and cayenne pepper

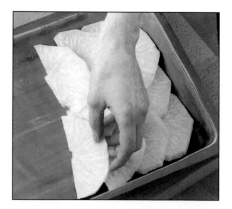

1 Preheat the oven to 375°F. Peel the celery root and cut into ¼-inch slices, immediately plunging them into a saucepan of cold water acidulated with the lemon juice.

2 Bring the water to a boil and simmer the celery root for 10–12 minutes until just tender. Drain and arrange the celery root in a shallow ovenproof dish.

3 Melt the butter in a small saucepan and fry the onion over low heat until soft but not browned. Stir in the flour, cook for 1 minute and then slowly stir in the milk to make a smooth sauce. Stir in the cheese, capers and seasoning to taste and then pour over the celery root. Cook in the oven for 15–20 minutes until the top is golden brown.

VARIATION
For a less strongly flavored dish, alternate the layers of celery root with potato. Slice the potato, cook until almost tender, then drain well before assembling the dish.

TOMATO AND BASIL TART

IN FRANCE, PATISSERIES DISPLAY MOUTH-WATERING SAVORY TARTS IN THEIR WINDOWS. THIS IS A VERY SIMPLE YET EXTREMELY TASTY TART MADE WITH RICH PIECRUST PASTRY, FILLED WITH SLICES OF MOZZARELLA CHEESE AND TOMATOES AND TOPPED WITH OLIVE OIL AND BASIL LEAVES.

SERVES FOUR

INGREDIENTS
    5 ounces young mozzarella,
        thinly sliced
    4 large tomatoes, thickly sliced
    about 10 basil leaves
    2 tablespoons olive oil
    2 garlic cloves, thinly sliced
    sea salt and freshly ground
        black pepper
For the pastry
    4 ounces all-purpose flour
    pinch of salt
    2 ounces butter or margarine
    1 egg yolk

1 To prepare the pastry, mix together the flour and salt, then rub in the butter or margarine and egg yolk. Add enough cold water to make a smooth dough and knead lightly on a floured surface. Place in a plastic bag and chill for about 1 hour.

2 Preheat the oven to 375°F. Remove pastry from the fridge and allow about 10 minutes for it to return to room temperature and then roll out into an 8-inch round. Press into the bottom of an 8-inch flan dish or pan. Prick all over with a fork and then bake in the oven for about 10 minutes until firm but not brown. Allow to cool slightly. Reduce the oven temperature to 350°F.

3 Arrange the mozzarella slices over the pastry base. On top, arrange a single layer of the sliced tomatoes, overlapping them slightly. Dip the basil leaves in olive oil and arrange them on the tomatoes.

4 Scatter the garlic on top, drizzle with the remaining olive oil and season with a little salt and a good sprinkling of black pepper. Bake for 40–45 minutes, until the tomatoes are well cooked. Serve hot.

VEGETABLES JULIENNE WITH A RED PEPPER COULIS

JUST THE RIGHT COURSE FOR THOSE WATCHING THEIR WEIGHT. CHOOSE A SELECTION OF AS MANY VEGETABLES AS YOU FEEL YOU CAN EAT.

SERVES TWO

INGREDIENTS

A selection of vegetables (choose from: carrots, turnips, asparagus, parsnips, zucchini, green beans, broccoli, salsify, cauliflower, snow peas)

For the red pepper coulis
1 small onion, chopped
1 garlic clove, crushed
1 tablespoon sunflower oil
1 tablespoon water
3 red bell peppers, roasted and skinned
8 tablespoons fromage blanc
squeeze of fresh lemon juice
salt and freshly ground black pepper
sprigs of fresh rosemary and thyme
2 bay leaves
fresh green herbs, to garnish

1 Prepare the vegetables by cutting them into thin fingers or small, bite-size pieces.

2 Make the coulis. Lightly sauté the onion and garlic in the oil and water for 3 minutes, then add the peppers and cook for another 2 minutes.

3 Purée the coulis in a food processor, then work in the fromage blanc, lemon juice and seasoning.

4 Boil some salted water with the fresh rosemary, thyme and bay leaves, and fit a steamer over the top.

5 Arrange the prepared vegetables on the steamer, placing the harder root vegetables at the bottom and steaming these for about 3 minutes.

6 Add the other vegetables according to their natural tenderness and cook for another 2–4 minutes.

7 Serve the vegetables on plates with the sauce to one side. Garnish with fresh green herbs, if you wish.

VARIATION

The red pepper coulis makes a wonderful sauce for many other dishes. Try it spooned over fresh pasta with lightly steamed or fried zucchini, or use it as a pouring sauce for savory filled crêpes.

BROCCOLI RISOTTO TORTE

*LIKE A SPANISH OMELET, THIS IS
A SAVORY CAKE SERVED IN
WEDGES. IT IS GOOD COLD OR
HOT, AND NEEDS ONLY A SALAD
AS AN ACCOMPANIMENT.*

SERVES SIX

INGREDIENTS
   8 ounces broccoli, cut into very small
      florets
   1 onion, chopped
   2 garlic cloves, crushed
   1 large yellow bell pepper, sliced
   2 tablespoons olive oil
   ¼ cup butter
   1¼ cups Arborio rice
   ½ cup dry white wine
   4½ cups vegetable stock
   salt and freshly ground black pepper
   ½ cup coarsely grated
      Parmesan cheese
   4 eggs, separated
   oil, for greasing
   sliced tomato and chopped parsley,
      to garnish

1 Blanch the broccoli for 3 minutes, then drain and reserve.

2 In a large saucepan, gently fry the onion, garlic and pepper in the oil and butter for 5 minutes, until they are soft.

3 Stir in the rice, cook for a minute, then pour in the wine. Cook, stirring the mixture, until the liquid is absorbed.

4 Pour in the stock, season well, bring to a boil, then lower to a simmer. Cook for 20 minutes, stirring occasionally.

5 Meanwhile, grease a deep 10-inch round cake pan and line the bottom with a circle of waxed paper. Preheat the oven to 350°F.

6 Stir the cheese into the rice, allow the mixture to cool for 5 minutes, then beat in the egg yolks.

7 Whisk the egg whites until they form soft peaks and carefully fold into the rice. Turn into the prepared pan and bake for about 1 hour, until risen, golden brown and slightly wobbly in the center.

8 Allow the torte to cool in the pan, then chill if serving cold. Run a knife around the edge of the pan and shake out onto a serving plate. If desired, garnish with sliced tomato and chopped parsley.

VEGETABLE AND HERB KEBABS WITH GREEN PEPPERCORN SAUCE

OTHER VEGETABLES CAN BE INCLUDED IN THESE KEBABS, DEPENDING ON WHAT IS AVAILABLE AT THE TIME. THE GREEN PEPPERCORN SAUCE IS ALSO AN EXCELLENT ACCOMPANIMENT TO MANY OTHER DISHES.

SERVES FOUR

INGREDIENTS

   8 bamboo skewers soaked in water for
    1 hour
   24 mushrooms
   16 cherry tomatoes
   16 large basil leaves
   16 thick slices of zucchini
   16 large mint leaves
   16 squares of red bell pepper
To baste
   ½ cup melted butter
   1 clove garlic, peeled and crushed
   1 tablespoon crushed green peppercorns
   salt
For the green peppercorn sauce
   ¼ cup butter
   3 tablespoons brandy
   1 cup heavy cream
   1 teaspoon crushed green peppercorns

1 Thread the vegetables and herbs onto bamboo skewers: place the basil leaves next to the tomatoes, and wrap mint leaves around the zucchini slices.

2 Mix the basting ingredients and baste the kebabs thoroughly. Place the skewers on a grill or under the broiler, turning and basting regularly until the vegetables are just cooked, about 5–7 minutes.

3 Heat the butter for the sauce in a frying pan, then add the brandy and light it. When the flames have died down, stir in the cream and the peppercorns. Cook for approximately 2 minutes, stirring constantly. Serve the kebabs with the green peppercorn sauce.

FESTIVE LENTIL AND NUT ROAST

SERVE WITH VEGETARIAN GRAVY,
CRANBERRIES AND FRENCH
PARSLEY.

SERVES SIX TO EIGHT

INGREDIENTS
⅔ cup red lentils
1 cup hazelnuts
1 cup walnuts
1 large carrot
2 celery stalks
1 large onion, sliced
4 ounces mushrooms
¼ cup butter
2 teaspoons mild curry powder
2 tablespoons ketchup
2 tbsp soy sauce
1 egg, beaten
2 teaspoons salt
4 tablespoons chopped fresh parsley
⅔ cup water

1 Soak the lentils for 1 hour in cold water, then drain well. Grind the nuts in a food processor until very fine but not too smooth. Set the nuts aside.

2 Chop the carrot, celery, onion and mushrooms into small chunks, then process them in a food processor or blender until they are finely chopped.

3 Fry the vegetables gently in the butter for 5 minutes, then stir in the curry powder and cook for a minute. Cool.

4 Mix the lentils with the nuts, vegetables and remaining ingredients.

5 Grease and line the bottom and sides of a long 2-pound loaf pan with waxed paper or a sheet of foil. Press the mixture into the pan. Preheat the oven to 375°F.

6 Bake for 1–1¼ hours, until just firm, covering the top with a buttered piece of waxed paper or foil if it starts to burn. Let the mixture stand for about 15 minutes before you turn it out and peel off the paper. It will be fairly soft when cut, as it is a moist loaf.

VEGETARIAN GRAVY

MAKE UP A LARGE BATCH AND
FREEZE IT IN SMALL CONTAINERS
READY TO REHEAT AND SERVE.

MAKES ABOUT 1 QUART

INGREDIENTS
1 large red onion, sliced
3 turnips, sliced
3 celery stalks, sliced
4 ounces white mushrooms, halved
2 whole garlic cloves
6 tablespoons sunflower oil
6 cups vegetable stock or water
3 tablespoons soy sauce
generous pinch of granulated sugar
salt and freshly ground black pepper

1 Cook the vegetables and garlic with the oil in a large saucepan over medium high heat, stirring occasionally, until nicely browned but not singed. This should take 15-20 minutes.

2 Add the stock or water and soy sauce, bring to a boil, then cover and simmer for another 20 minutes.

3 Purée the vegetables, adding a little of the stock, and return them to the pan by rubbing the pulp through a sieve with the back of a ladle or wooden spoon.

4 Taste for seasoning and add the sugar. Freeze at least half of the gravy to use later and reheat the rest to serve with rice and peas or the lentil and nut roast.

GREEK STUFFED VEGETABLES

VEGETABLES SUCH AS BELL PEPPERS MAKE WONDERFUL CONTAINERS FOR SAVORY FILLINGS. THICK, CREAMY GREEK YOGURT IS THE IDEAL ACCOMPANIMENT.

SERVES THREE TO SIX

INGREDIENTS
1 medium eggplant
1 large green bell pepper
2 large tomatoes
1 large onion, chopped
2 garlic cloves, crushed
3 tablespoons olive oil
1 cup brown rice
2½ cups vegetable stock
¾ cup pine nuts
⅓ cup currants
salt and freshly ground black pepper
3 tablespoons chopped fresh dill
3 tablespoons chopped fresh parsley
1 tablespoon chopped fresh mint
extra olive oil, to sprinkle
plain yogurt, to serve
fresh sprigs of dill

1 Halve the eggplant, scoop out the flesh with a sharp knife and chop finely. Salt the insides and leave to drain upside down for 20 minutes while you prepare the other ingredients.

2 Halve the pepper, seed and core. Cut the tops from the tomatoes, scoop out the insides and chop coarsely along with the tomato tops.

3 Fry the onion, garlic and chopped eggplant in the oil for 10 minutes, then stir in the rice and cook for 2 minutes.

4 Add the tomatoes, stock, pine nuts, currants and seasoning. Bring to a boil, cover and simmer for 15 minutes, then stir in the fresh herbs.

5 Blanch the eggplant and green pepper halves in boiling water for about 3 minutes, then drain them upside down.

6 Spoon the rice filling into all six vegetable containers and place in a lightly greased shallow ovenproof dish.

7 Heat the oven to 375°F. Drizzle some olive oil over the vegetables and bake for 25–30 minutes. Serve hot, topped with spoonfuls of plain yogurt and dill sprigs.

THAI NOODLES <u>WITH</u> GARLIC CHIVES

THIS RECIPE REQUIRES A LITTLE TIME FOR PREPARATION, BUT THE COOKING TIME IS VERY FAST. EVERYTHING IS COOKED SPEEDILY IN A HOT WOK AND SHOULD BE EATEN AT ONCE.

SERVES FOUR

INGREDIENTS
  12 ounces dried rice noodles
  ½-inch piece fresh ginger, grated
  2 tablespoons light soy sauce
  3 tablespoons vegetable oil
  2 garlic cloves, crushed
  1 large onion, cut into thin wedges
  4 ounces fried bean curd,
    thinly sliced
  1 green chili, seeded
    and finely sliced
  6 ounces bean sprouts
  4 ounces garlic chives, cut into
    2-inch lengths
  2 ounces roasted peanuts, ground
  2 tablespoons dark soy sauce
  2 tablespoons chopped fresh
    cilantro
  1 lemon, cut into wedges

1 Place the noodles in a large bowl, cover with warm water and soak for 20–30 minutes, then drain. Blend together the ginger, light soy sauce and 1 tablespoon of the oil in a bowl. Set aside for 10 minutes. Drain, reserving the marinade.

2 Heat 1 tablespoon of the oil in a wok or large frying pan. Fry the garlic for a few seconds, then remove from pan and discard.

3 Heat the remaining oil in the wok or frying pan and stir-fry the onion for 3–4 minutes until softened and tinged with brown. Add the bean curd and chili, stir-fry briefly and then add the noodles. Stir-fry for 4–5 minutes.

4 Stir in the bean sprouts, garlic chives and most of the ground peanuts, reserving a little for the garnish. Stir well, then add the dark soy sauce and the reserved marinade.

5 When hot, spoon onto serving plates and garnish with the remaining ground peanuts, cilantro and lemon wedges.

COOK'S TIP
This a vegetarian meal, however, thinly sliced pork or chicken could be used instead. Stir-fry it initially for 4–5 minutes.

SHEPHERDESS PIE

A NO-MEAT VERSION OF THE TIMELESS CLASSIC, THIS DISH CONTAINS NO DAIRY PRODUCTS, SO IS SUITABLE FOR VEGANS.

SERVES SIX TO EIGHT

INGREDIENTS

    2 pounds potatoes
    3 tablespoons extra-virgin olive oil
    salt and freshly ground black pepper
    1 large onion, chopped
    1 green bell pepper, chopped
    2 carrots, coarsely grated
    2 garlic cloves
    3 tablespoons sunflower oil or
      margarine
    4 ounces mushrooms, chopped
    2 cans (14 ounces each) aduki beans
    2½ cups vegetable stock
    1 teaspoon vegetable yeast extract
    2 bay leaves
    1 teaspoon dried Italian herbs
    dried bread crumbs or chopped nuts,
      to sprinkle

1 Boil the potatoes in their skins until tender, then drain, reserving a little of the water to moisten them.

2 Mash well, mixing in the olive oil and seasoning until you have a smooth purée.

3 Gently fry the onion, pepper, carrots and garlic in the sunflower oil or margarine for about 5 minutes, until they are soft. Preheat the broiler.

4 Stir in the mushrooms and drained beans and cook for another 2 minutes, then add the stock, yeast extract, bay leaves and mixed herbs. Simmer for 15 minutes.

5 Remove the bay leaves and empty the vegetables into a shallow ovenproof dish. Spoon on the potatoes in dollops and sprinkle with the bread crumbs or nuts. Broil until golden brown.

ROAST ASPARAGUS CRÊPES

ROAST ASPARAGUS IS DELICIOUS AND GOOD ENOUGH TO EAT JUST AS IT COMES. HOWEVER, FOR A REALLY SPLENDID STARTER, TRY THIS SIMPLE RECIPE. EITHER MAKE SIX LARGE OR TWICE AS MANY COCKTAIL-SIZE PANCAKES TO USE WITH SMALLER STEMS OF ASPARAGUS.

SERVES SIX (as a starter)

INGREDIENTS
   1 pound fresh asparagus
   6–8 tablespoons olive oil
   6 ounces mascarpone cheese
   4 tablespoons light cream
   1 ounce Parmesan cheese, grated
   sea salt
For the pancakes
   6 ounces all-purpose flour
   2 eggs
   1½ cups milk
   vegetable oil, for frying
   pinch of salt

1 To make the pancake batter, mix the flour with the salt in a large bowl, food processor or blender, then add the eggs and milk and beat or process to make a smooth, fairly thin, batter.

2 Heat a little oil in a large frying pan and add a small amount of batter, swirling the pan to coat the base evenly. Cook over moderate heat for about 1 minute, then flip over and cook the other side until golden. Set aside and cook the rest of the pancakes in the same way; the mixture makes about six large or 12 smaller pancakes.

3 Preheat the oven to 350°F and lightly grease a large shallow ovenproof dish or roasting pan with some of the olive oil.

4 Trim the asparagus by placing on a board and cutting off the bases. Using a small sharp knife, peel away the woody ends, if necessary.

5 Arrange the asparagus in a single layer in the dish, trickle over the remaining olive oil, rolling the asparagus to coat each one thoroughly. Sprinkle with a little salt and then roast in the oven for about 8–12 minutes until tender (the cooking time depends on the stem thickness).

6 Blend the mascarpone cheese with the cream and Parmesan cheese and spread a generous tablespoonful over each of the pancakes, leaving a little extra for the topping. Preheat the broiler.

7 Divide the asparagus spears among the pancakes, roll up and arrange in a single layer in an ovenproof dish. Spoon over the remaining cheese mixture and then place under a moderate broiler for 4–5 minutes, until heated through and golden brown. Serve at once.

SALADS &
SIDE DISHES
~

HASSELBACK POTATOES

A VERY UNUSUAL WAY WITH POTATOES. EACH POTATO HALF IS SLICED ALMOST TO THE BASE AND THEN ROASTED WITH OIL AND BUTTER. THE CRISPY POTATOES ARE THEN COATED IN AN ORANGE GLAZE AND RETURNED TO THE OVEN UNTIL DEEP GOLDEN BROWN AND CRUNCHY.

SERVES FOUR TO SIX

INGREDIENTS
  4 large potatoes
  1 ounce butter, melted
  3 tablespoons olive oil
  freshly ground black pepper
For the glaze
  juice of 1 orange
  grated rind of ½ orange
  1 tablespoon brown sugar

1 Preheat the oven to 375°F. Cut each potato in half lengthwise, place flat-side down and then cut down as if making very thin slices, but leaving the bottom ½ inch intact.

2 Place the potatoes in a large roasting dish. Using a pastry brush coat the potatoes generously with the melted butter and pour the olive oil over the bottom and around the potatoes.

3 Bake the potatoes in the oven for 40–50 minutes until they begin to brown. Baste occasionally during cooking.

4 Meanwhile, place the orange juice, orange rind and sugar in a small saucepan and heat gently, stirring until the sugar has dissolved. Simmer for 3–4 minutes until the glaze is fairly thick and then remove from the heat.

5 When the potatoes begin to brown, brush all over with the orange glaze and return to the oven to roast for a further 15 minutes or until the potatoes are a deep golden brown. Serve at once.

KALE WITH PARMESAN AND GARLIC

KALE IS A ROBUST, FULL-BODIED TYPE OF CABBAGE. IT HAS A VERY PRONOUNCED FLAVOR AND IS GOOD WHEN COOKED WITH OTHER STRONG-FLAVORED INGREDIENTS SUCH AS ONIONS, GARLIC AND PARMESAN CHEESE. IT DOES NOT NEED LONG COOKING AS THE LEAVES ARE QUITE TENDER.

SERVES FOUR

INGREDIENTS
    3 tablespoons olive oil
    2 garlic cloves, crushed
    4 scallions, sliced
    12 ounces curly kale, thinly sliced,
        tough stalk removed
    2 ounces Parmesan cheese, grated
    salt and freshly ground black pepper
    shavings of Parmesan cheese,
        to garnish

1 Heat the olive oil in a large saucepan or wok and fry the garlic gently for a few seconds. Add the scallions, stir-fry for 2 minutes and then add the kale.

2 Stir-fry for a few minutes so that the kale is coated in oil, and then add about ¼ cup water. Bring to a boil, cover and simmer until the kale is tender. Stir occasionally during cooking and do not allow the pan to boil dry.

3 Bring the liquid to the boil and allow the excess to evaporate and then stir in the Parmesan cheese. Serve at once with extra shavings of cheese, if liked.

PEAS WITH BABY ONIONS AND CREAM

IDEALLY, USE FRESH PEAS AND FRESH BABY ONIONS. FROZEN PEAS ARE AN ACCEPTABLE SUBSTITUTE IF FRESH ONES AREN'T AVAILABLE, BUT FROZEN ONIONS TEND TO BE INSIPID AND ARE NOT WORTH USING. ALTERNATELY, USE THE WHITE PART OF SCALLIONS.

SERVES FOUR

INGREDIENTS

6 ounces baby onions
½ ounce butter
2 pounds fresh peas (about 12 ounces shelled or frozen)
⅔ cup heavy cream
½ ounce all-purpose flour
2 teaspoons chopped fresh parsley
1–2 tablespoons lemon juice (optional)
salt and freshly ground black pepper

1 Peel the onions and halve them if necessary. Melt the butter in a flame-proof casserole and fry the onions for 5–6 minutes over moderate heat, until they begin to be flecked with brown.

3 Using a small whisk, blend the cream with the flour. Remove the pan from the heat and stir in the combined cream and flour, parsley and seasoning to taste.

4 Cook over low heat for about 3–4 minutes, until the sauce is thick. Taste and adjust the seasoning; add a little lemon juice to sharpen, if liked.

2 Add the peas and stir-fry for a few minutes. Add ¼ cup water and bring to a boil. Partially cover and simmer for about 10 minutes until both the peas and onions are tender. There should be a thin layer of water on the bottom of the pan – add a little more water if necessary or if there is too much liquid, remove the lid and increase the heat until the liquid is reduced.

WAX BEANS WITH GARLIC

DELICATE AND FRESH TASTING FLAGEOLET BEANS AND GARLIC ADD A DISTINCT FRENCH FLAVOR TO THIS SIMPLE SIDE DISH. SERVE TO ACCOMPANY ROAST LAMB OR VEAL.

SERVES FOUR

INGREDIENTS

   8 ounces flageolet beans
   1 tablespoon olive oil
   1 ounce butter
   1 onion, finely chopped
   1–2 garlic cloves, crushed
   3–4 tomatoes, peeled and chopped
   12 ounces wax beans, prepared and
     sliced
   ⅔ cup white wine
   ⅔ cup vegetable stock
   2 tablespoons chopped fresh parsley
   salt and freshly ground black pepper

1 Place the flageolet beans in a large saucepan of water, bring to a boil and simmer for ¾–1 hour until tender. Drain.

2 Heat the oil and butter in a large frying pan and sauté the onion and garlic for 3–4 minutes until soft. Add the chopped tomatoes and continue cooking over low heat until they are soft.

3 Stir the flageolet beans into the onion and tomato mixture, then add the wax beans, wine, stock, and a little salt. Stir well. Cover and simmer for 5–10 minutes until the wax beans are tender.

4 Increase the heat to reduce the liquid, then stir in the parsley and season with a little more salt, if necessary, and pepper.

SHIITAKE FRIED RICE

SHIITAKE MUSHROOMS HAVE A STRONG MEATY MUSHROOMY AROMA AND FLAVOR. THIS IS A VERY EASY RECIPE TO MAKE, AND ALTHOUGH IT IS A SIDE DISH IT CAN ALMOST BE A MEAL IN ITSELF.

SERVES FOUR

INGREDIENTS
2 eggs
3 tablespoons vegetable oil
12 ounces shiitake mushrooms
8 scallions, sliced diagonally
1 garlic clove, crushed
½ green bell pepper, chopped
1 ounce butter
12 ounces cooked long grain rice
1 tablespoon medium dry sherry
2 tablespoons dark soy sauce
1 tablespoon chopped fresh cilantro
salt

1 Beat the eggs with 1 tablespoon of cold water and season with a little salt.

2 Heat 1 tablespoon of the oil in a wok or large frying pan, pour in the eggs and cook to make a large omelet. Lift the sides of the omelet and tilt the wok so that the uncooked egg can run underneath and be cooked. Roll up the omelet and slice thinly.

3 Remove and discard the mushroom stalks if tough and slice the caps thinly, halving them if they are large.

4 Heat 1 tablespoon of the remaining oil in the wok and stir-fry the scallions and garlic for 3–4 minutes until softened but not brown. Transfer them to a plate using a slotted spoon.

5 Add the pepper, stir-fry for about 2–3 minutes, then add the butter and the remaining 1 tablespoon of oil. As the butter begins to sizzle, add the mushrooms and stir-fry over moderate heat for 3–4 minutes until soft.

6 Loosen the rice grains as much as possible. Pour the sherry over the mushrooms and then stir in the rice.

7 Heat the rice over moderate heat, stirring all the time to prevent the rice sticking. If the rice seems very dry, add a little more oil. Stir in the reserved onions and omelet slices, the soy sauce and cilantro. Cook for a few minutes until heated through and serve.

COOK'S TIP
Unlike risotto, for which rice is cooked along with the other ingredients. Chinese fried rice is always made using cooked rice. If you use 6–8 ounces uncooked long grain, you will get about 16–20 ounces of cooked rice, enough for four people.

GLAZED CARROTS WITH CIDER

THIS RECIPE IS EXTREMELY SIMPLE TO MAKE. THE CARROTS ARE COOKED IN THE MINIMUM OF LIQUID TO BRING OUT THE BEST OF THEIR FLAVOR, AND THE CIDER ADDS A PLEASANT SHARPNESS.

SERVES FOUR

INGREDIENTS
1 pound young carrots
1 ounce butter
1 tablespoon brown sugar
½ cup cider
4 tablespoons vegetable stock or water
1 teaspoon French mustard
1 tablespoon finely chopped fresh
  parsley

1 Trim the tops and bottoms off the carrots. Peel or scrape them. Using a sharp knife cut the carrots into julienne.

2 Melt the butter in a saucepan, add the carrots and sauté for 4–5 minutes, stirring frequently. Sprinkle over the sugar and cook, stirring for 1 minute or until the sugar has dissolved.

3 Add the cider and stock or water, bring to a boil and stir in the French mustard. Partially cover the pan and simmer for about 10–12 minutes until the carrots are just tender. Remove the lid and continue cooking until the liquid has reduced to a thick sauce.

4 Remove the saucepan from the heat, stir in the parsley and then spoon into a warmed serving dish. Serve as an accompaniment to broiled meat or fish or with a vegetarian dish.

COOK'S TIP
If the carrots are cooked before the liquid in the saucepan has reduced, transfer the carrots to a serving dish and rapidly boil the liquid until thick. Pour over the carrots and sprinkle with parsley.

CARROT, APPLE AND ORANGE COLESLAW

THIS DISH IS AS DELICIOUS AS IT IS EASY TO MAKE. THE GARLIC AND HERB DRESSING ADDS THE NECESSARY CONTRAST TO THE SWEETNESS OF THE SALAD.

SERVES FOUR

INGREDIENTS
12 ounces young carrots,
  finely grated
2 eating apples
1 tablespoon lemon juice
1 large orange
For the dressing
3 tablespoons olive oil
4 tablespoons sunflower oil
3 tablespoons lemon juice
1 garlic clove, crushed
4 tablespoons plain yogurt
1 tablespoon chopped mixed fresh
  herbs: tarragon, parsley, chives
salt and freshly ground black pepper

1 Place the carrots in a large serving bowl. Quarter the apples, remove the core and then slice thinly. Sprinkle with the lemon juice to prevent them discoloring and then add to the carrots.

2 Using a sharp knife, remove the peel and pith from the oranges and then separate into segments.

3 To make the dressing, place all the ingredients in a jar with a tight-fitting lid and shake vigorously to blend.

4 Just before serving, pour the dressing over the salad and toss well together.

CRUNCHY CABBAGE SALAD WITH PESTO MAYONNAISE

BOTH THE PESTO AND THE MAYONNAISE CAN BE MADE FOR THIS DISH. HOWEVER, IF TIME IS SHORT, YOU CAN BUY THEM BOTH READY-PREPARED AND IT WILL TASTE JUST AS GOOD.

SERVES FOUR TO SIX

INGREDIENTS
  1 small or ½ medium white cabbage
  3–4 carrots, grated
  4 scallions, finely sliced
  1–1½ ounces pine nuts
  1 tablespoon chopped fresh mixed
    herbs; parsley, basil and chervil
For the pesto dressing
  1 egg yolk
  about 2 teaspoons lemon juice
  ⅞ cup sunflower oil
  2 teaspoons pesto
  4 tablespoons plain yogurt
  salt and freshly ground black pepper

1 To make the mayonnaise, place the egg yolk in a blender or food processor and process with the lemon juice. With the machine running, very slowly add the oil, pouring it more quickly as the mayonnaise emulsifies. Season to taste with salt and pepper and a little more lemon juice if necessary. Alternately, make by hand using a balloon whisk.

2 Spoon 5 tablespoons of mayonnaise into a bowl and stir in the pesto and yogurt, beating well to make a fairly thin dressing. (The remaining mayonnaise will keep for about 3–4 weeks in a screw-top jar in the fridge.)

3 Using a food processor or a sharp knife, thinly slice the cabbage and place in a large salad bowl.

4 Add the carrots and scallions, together with the herbs and pine nuts, mixing thoroughly with your hands. Stir the pesto dressing into the salad or serve separately in a small dish if preferred.

PEPERONATA <u>WITH</u> RAISINS

*SLICED ROASTED PEPPERS IN
DRESSING WITH VINEGAR-SOAKED
RAISINS MAKE A TASTY SIDE
SALAD THAT COMPLEMENTS MANY
OTHER DISHES.*

SERVES TWO TO FOUR

INGREDIENTS
   6 tablespoons sliced peppers in olive
   oil, drained
   1 tablespoon chopped onion
   2 tablespoons balsamic vinegar
   3 tablespoons raisins
   2 tablespoons chopped fresh parsley
   ground black pepper

1 Toss the peppers with the onion and let
steep for an hour.

2 Put the vinegar and raisins in a small
saucepan and heat for a minute, then
let cool.

3 Mix all the ingredients together
thoroughly and spoon into a serving bowl.
Serve lightly chilled.

COOK'S TIP
Peperonata is one of the classic Italian
antipasto dishes, served at the start of
each meal with crusty bread to mop up
the delicious juices. Try serving shavings
of fresh Parmesan cheese alongside, or
buy a good selection of green and black
olives to accompany the peperonata.
Small baby tomatoes will complete the
antipasto.

GREEN BEAN SALAD

ALTHOUGH BEAN SALADS ARE DELICIOUS SERVED WITH A SIMPLE VINAIGRETTE DRESSING, THIS DISH IS A LITTLE MORE ELABORATE. IT DOES, HOWEVER, ENHANCE THE FRESH FLAVOR OF THE BEANS.

SERVES FOUR

INGREDIENTS
    1 pound green beans
    1 tablespoon olive oil
    1 ounce butter
    ½ garlic clove, crushed
    2 ounces fresh white bread crumbs
    1 tablespoon chopped fresh parsley
    1 egg, hard-boiled and finely chopped
    For the dressing
    2 tablespoons olive oil
    2 tablespoons sunflower oil
    2 teaspoons white wine vinegar
    ½ garlic clove, crushed
    ¼ teaspoon Dijon mustard
    pinch of sugar
    pinch of salt

1 Trim the green beans and cook in boiling salted water for 5–6 minutes until tender. Drain the beans and refresh them under cold running water and place in a serving bowl.

2 Make the salad dressing by blending the oils, vinegar, garlic, mustard, sugar and salt thoroughly together. Pour over the beans and toss to mix.

COOK'S TIP
For a more substantial salad, boil about 1 pound scrubbed new potatoes until tender, cool and then cut them into bite-size chunks. Stir into the green beans and then add the dressing.

3 Heat the oil and butter in a frying pan and fry the garlic for 1 minute. Stir in the bread crumbs and fry over moderate heat for about 3–4 minutes until golden brown, stirring frequently.

4 Remove the pan from the heat and stir in the parsley and then the egg. Sprinkle the breadcrumb mixture over the green beans. Serve warm or at room temperature.

RADISH, MANGO AND APPLE SALAD

RADISH IS AVAILABLE ALL YEAR THROUGH AND THIS SALAD CAN BE SERVED ANY TIME OF YEAR, WITH ITS CLEAN, CRISP TASTES AND MELLOW FLAVORS. SERVE WITH SMOKED FISH, SUCH AS ROLLS OF SMOKED SALMON OR WITH CONTINENTAL HAM OR SALAMI.

SERVES FOUR

INGREDIENTS
    10–15 radishes
    1 eating apple, peeled cored and
      thinly sliced
    2 celery stalks, thinly sliced
    1 small ripe mango, peeled and cut
      into small chunks
For the dressing
    ½ cup sour cream
    2 teaspoons creamed horseradish
    1 tablespoon chopped fresh dill
    salt and fresh ground black pepper
    sprig of dill, to garnish

3 Cut through the mango lengthwise either side of the pit. Make even criss-cross cuts through each side section. Take each one and bend it back to separate the cubes. Remove the mango cubes with a small knife and add to the bowl. Pour the dressing over the vegetables and fruit and stir gently so that all the ingredients are coated in the dressing. When ready to serve, spoon the salad into an attractive salad bowl and garnish with a sprig of dill.

1 To prepare the dressing, blend together the sour cream, horseradish and dill in a small jug or bowl and season with a little salt and pepper.

2 Remove the ends of the radishes and then slice them thinly. Add to a bowl together with the thinly sliced apple and celery.

POTATO SALAD WITH CURRY PLANT MAYONNAISE

POTATO SALAD CAN BE MADE WELL IN ADVANCE AND IS THEREFORE A USEFUL BUFFET DISH. ITS POPULARITY MEANS THAT THERE ARE VERY RARELY ANY LEFTOVERS.

SERVES SIX

INGREDIENTS
  salt
  2 pounds new potatoes,
   in skins
  1¼ cups mayonnaise
  6 curry-plant leaves, roughly chopped
  black pepper
  mixed lettuce or other salad greens, to
   serve

1 Place the potatoes in a pan of salted water and boil for 15 minutes, or until tender. Drain and place in a large bowl to cool slightly.

2 Mix the mayonnaise with the curry-plant leaves and black pepper. Stir these into the potatoes while they are still warm. Let cool, then serve on a bed of mixed lettuce or other assorted salad leaves.

GARDEN SALAD <u>AND</u> GARLIC CROSTINI

DRESS A COLORFUL MIXTURE OF
SALAD LEAVES WITH GOOD OLIVE
OIL AND FRESH LEMON JUICE.

SERVES FOUR TO SIX

INGREDIENTS
3 thick slices day-old bread
½ cup extra-virgin olive oil
garlic clove, cut
½ small head romaine lettuce
½ small oak leaf lettuce
2 tablespoons arugula leaves or watercress
2 tablespoons fresh flat-leaf parsley
a few leaves and flowers of nasturtium
flowers of pansy and pot marigold
a handful of young dandelion leaves
sea salt flakes and freshly ground
  black pepper
juice of 1 fresh lemon

1 Cut the bread into medium-size dice
about ½-inch square.

2 Heat half the oil gently in a frying pan
and fry the bread cubes in it, tossing
them until they are well coated and lightly
browned. Remove and cool.

3 Rub the inside of a large salad bowl
with the garlic and discard. Pour the rest
of the oil into the bottom of the bowl.

4 Wash, dry and tear the leaves into bite-
size pieces and pile them into the bowl.
Season with salt and pepper. Cover and
keep chilled until ready to serve.

5 To serve, toss the leaves in the oil at
the bottom of the bowl, then sprinkle with
the lemon juice and toss again. Scatter
over the crostini and serve immediately.

INDEX